'With the Windrush increas[ing] the migration of West India[ns in the] post-war period, there is an [awareness] that the Caribbean presence [in fact] stretches back centuries. This book must be welcomed for drawing attention to the historical contributions made by a range of remarkable women and men, who have impacted on so many spheres of British life. These often overlooked or untold pre-Windrush stories resonate with me personally, knowing that my mother was a nurse in the UK in the 1930s, my father (a lifelong friend of fellow Trinidadians Padmore, James and Constantine, who feature within these pages) was a doctor in 1920s Walthamstow, and my maternal grandfather was a delegate at the 1900 First Pan-African Conference in London, having come from Dominica to study Law. Before Windrush: West Indians in Britain *points the way towards ensuring that all those it names are rightfully given credit due, while perhaps inspiring readers to seek out others also deserving of greater attention.*'

Margaret Busby

'The publication of Before Windrush: West Indians in Britain by Asher & Martin Hoyles is very timely, considering the Windrush Scandal of April 2018 which exposed the level of ignorance about the history of the Windrush Generation. With the government adopting national Windrush Day and increasing pressure for the national curriculum to reflect more black and migration history, this will be a valuable resource for schools and the wider public, providing a deeper understanding of the foundation and roots of the Windrush Generation.'

Patrick Vernon OBE (Founder of Windrush Day)

'The contribution of those of African heritage is often overlooked in the history of Britain. This telling of their stories through poetry and prose uniquely rectifies this omission revealing the legacy of the many West Indians who came to these shores and the part they played in helping to make Britain the country it is today.'

Oku Ekpenyon MBE (Chair of Slavery Memorial 2007)

'The history of Windrush is now a household tale in Britain. Caribbean and African history in Britain before Windrush has been largely whitewashed and marginalised. *Before Windrush* adds a crucial dimension to history, recording forgotten annals of black achievement that impacted on war, sport, and social advancement in all areas of public life. Martin and Asher Hoyles' work brings to life the achievements of men and women who triumphed over racism in their efforts to change the texture of human interaction in Britain – both for themselves and for those similarly challenged by inequality and oppression. Their stories, told in vibrant prose and poetry, are a stirring page-turner from Hansib Publications for this and future generations.'

Shango Baku (Rastafari Actor/Writer)

'*Before Windrush* is an important contribution to the history of black people in the UK, showing the vital contribution that our forefathers and foremothers have made to this country. I come from a 300-year-old established black community in Liverpool, the oldest in Europe, yet our history is rarely told. Today, in the aftermath of George Floyd's murder, institutional racism is once again at the forefront of public consciousness and there is no better time than now to push for the full contribution of black people to the creation of this country to become mainstream. I'd urge you to read this informative book and carry on exploring our hidden history until it is hidden no more.'

Kim Johnson (MP for Liverpool Riverside)

BEFORE WINDRUSH

West Indians in Britain

Asher & Martin Hoyles

HANSIB

Celebrating 50 years of publishing 1970–2020

First published in Great Britain by Hansib Publications in 2020

Hansib Publications Limited
P.O. Box 226, Hertford, SG14 3WY

info@hansibpublications.com
www.hansibpublications.com

Copyright © Asher & Martin Hoyles, 2020

FRONT COVER IMAGES
Top row (L-R): Norman Manley, Amy Ashwood Garvey, C.L.R. James, Fanny Eaton; *middle row (L-R)*: Learie Constantine, Jean Rhys; *bottom row (L-R)*: Annie Brewster, George Padmore, Una Marson, Billy Strachan.

ISBN 978-1-912662-29-6

A CIP catalogue record for this book
is available from the British Library

All rights reserved.
Without limiting the rights under copyright reserved above, no part of this publication may be reproduced, stored in or introduced into a retrieval system, or transmitted, in any form or by any means (electronic, mechanical, photocopying, recording or otherwise), without the prior written permission of both the copyright owner and the publisher of this book.

Design & Production by Hansib Publications Ltd
Printed in Great Britain

*To Arif Ali on the 50th Anniversary of
Hansib Publications (1970-2020)*

Also by Asher & Martin Hoyles

Caribbean Publishing in Britain, 2011

Dyslexia from a Cultural Perspective, 2007

Moving Voices: Black Performance Poetry, 2002

Remember Me: Achievements of Mixed Race People, Past and Present, 1999

Acknowledgements

We would like to thank the following for their help and encouragement in writing this book:
Arif and Kash Ali, Shango Baku, Margaret Busby, Oku Ekpenyon, Amelia Gentleman, Kim Johnson, David Lammy, Arthur Torrington, Patrick Vernon.

Picture Credits

Princeton University Art Museum, (Fanny Eaton);
The Fitzwilliam Museum, (Fanny Eaton);
Courtesy of Barts Health NHS Trust Archives and Museums (Annie Brewster)

Contents

Preface by Arif Ali 13
Introduction 17

SLAVES AND SERVANTS

Francis Barber (c.1742-1801) Jamaica 22
Jonathan Strong (c.1748-1773) Barbados 25
Mary Prince (1788-c.1833) Bermuda 27
John Edmonstone (c.1800-1843) Guyana 29
Fanny Eaton (1835-1924) Jamaica 31

Dare to Dream the Dream – Asher 36

NURSES AND DOCTORS

Mary Seacole (1805-1881) Jamaica 38
Annie Brewster (1858-1902) St Vincent 41
John Alcindor (1873-1924) Trinidad 44
Harold Moody (1882-1947) Jamaica 47

Stolen Identity – Asher 51

POLITICAL ACTIVISTS

William Davidson (1786-1820) Jamaica 54
Robert Wedderburn (1762-c.1835) Jamaica 56
Celestine Edwards (1858-1894) Dominica 59

Henry Sylvester Williams (1869-1911) Trinidad 62
Marcus Garvey (1887-1940) Jamaica 65
Amy Ashwood Garvey (1895-1969) Jamaica 69
T. Ras Makonnen (1900-1983) Guyana 72
George Padmore (1902-1959) Trinidad 76
Una Marson (1905-1965) Jamaica 80

Raise Up The Low – Asher 86
The Spoken Word – Asher 89

SOLDIERS AND AIRMEN

Norman Manley (1893-1969) Jamaica 93
Cy Grant (1919-2010) Guyana 97
Arthur Wint (1920-1992) Jamaica 100
Billy Strachan (1921-1998) Jamaica 103

Don't Attack Iraq – Asher 107

SPORTSMEN

Andrew Watson (1856-1921) Guyana 112
Learie Constantine (1901-1971) Trinidad 114
Jack London (1905-1966) Guyana 119

The Talking Book – Asher 122

WRITERS

Jean Rhys (1890-1979) Dominica 126
Eric Walrond (1898-1966) Guyana 129
C. L. R. James (1901-1989) Trinidad 135

Select Bibliography 140

Preface

It is impossible to mark any occasion or event that falls (or would have fallen) in the year 2020 without making reference to the global pandemic. None of us has remained unaffected by this tragic event. As we all take tentative steps out of lockdown or quarantine, we look to an uncertain future and try to come to terms with the 'new normal'. Life may never be the same again and it will be a long time before the spectre of the virus is no longer an imminent threat.

Set against the backdrop of COVID-19, I am mindful that marking the 50th anniversary of the founding of Hansib Publications pales into relative insignificance. However, as much as future generations will refer to 2020 as the year of COVID-19, there are several 2020 events which will undoubtedly shape forthcoming impressions of our world and the future relationships of its inhabitants.

Since its 1970 inception, Hansib Publications has catered for the interests and needs of Britain's Caribbean, African and South Asian heritage communities. Through its newspapers and magazines in the seventies, eighties and nineties – through titles such as *West Indian Digest*, *Caribbean Times*, *Asian Times* and *African Times* – Hansib has campaigned for, and supported, Britain's visible minority communities. From challenging inequality in provision of education and accommodation, racial injustice within the legal system and discrimination in employment; deaths in custody, police brutality and the racially motivated murders of the likes of Kelso Cochrane, Rolan Adams and Stephen Lawrence. We also take pride in the role our organisation played in the elevation of the first Black Members of Parliament, and for the years of supporting the Notting Hill Carnival and promoting tourism and investment in the Caribbean, to name just a few highlights. In all of these major issues, plus many, many more, Hansib Publications has either been at the forefront or, at least, influential.

Since the early 1980s, Hansib has also published nearly three hundred books; many of which have become recommended texts on a number of college and university courses in the United Kingdom, the Caribbean and North America. We also like to believe most of our books may also have entertained as well as informed and educated our multi-cultural readership.

In 1948, the ship, *Empire Windrush* brought the first large group of Caribbean people to the UK. Many were answering the call from Britain seeking workers in the aftermath of the Second World War and the subsequent labour shortages, particularly in the fledgling National Health Service. As part of the British Commonwealth, citizens of the English-speaking Caribbean nations were automatically British citizens who were free to permanently live and work in the UK. And the 'Windrush Generation' refers to those who arrived in the UK from Caribbean countries from 1948 to 1973. I, myself, arrived in England from pre-independence British Guiana (Guyana since 1966) in September 1957.

The British Nationality Act 1948 gave citizenship of the UK and colonies to all people living in the United Kingdom and its colonies, and the right of entry and settlement in the UK. The 1971 Immigration Act ruled that Commonwealth citizens already living in the UK were given indefinite leave to remain.

The now notorious 'Windrush Scandal' came to public attention in 2018 following a campaign mounted by Caribbean diplomats to the UK and some British parliamentarians, among others. This political and human rights outrage occurred when people of Caribbean heritage had been wrongly detained, denied legal rights, threatened with deportation and, in a number of cases, deported from the UK by the Home Office. Some of those affected by these pernicious actions also lost their jobs, their homes (sometimes both), or were denied benefits or medical care to which they were entitled. The scandal has since prompted a wider debate about British immigration policy and Home Office practice.

While the momentous arrival of the *Empire Windrush* is well documented, along with many stories of the ground-breaking and epoch-defining Windrush Generation and, in turn, the subsequent injustices of the Windrush Scandal, what is little-known are the stories of those West Indians who were in Britain before *Windrush*.

Since at least the eighteenth century, people of African/Caribbean heritage have been part of the British landscape – and since the late nineteenth century, increasingly more influential.

Before Windrush: West Indians in Britain is a collection of biographies that sheds light on this much-overlooked presence and aims to provide an essential accompaniment to an obscured and frequently neglected area of British history. The book's sub-title, incidentally, pays homage to a series of Hansib books, first published in 1973, entitled, *West Indians in Britain*, which were volumes of biographies of members of the community at the time.

This sterling work by Asher and Martin Hoyles marks the fifth title authored by this husband and wife team and published by Hansib. Since 1999, their names, either jointly or individually, have been a regular feature among our list of published authors.

I hope that this important addition to the Hansib Publications catalogue of work will serve as a centrepiece in the debate which succeeding generations of academics and activists will continue and serve as a permanent reminder of the presence of people from the Caribbean in Britain before 1948 and who, similarly, made significant contributions to many areas of British society.

Arif Ali
Founder, Hansib Publications
September 2020

Introduction

'Our love of England and our wholehearted acceptance of English life and customs, at the expense of everything African, blinded us to many things. It has even made us seem a trifle absurd and ridiculous in the eyes of our neighbours. But the absurdity of our position - an ostrich-like one – was not revealed to us until we began to travel.' **Eric Walrond** *White Man, What Now?* The Spectator 5 April 1935

> Little brown girl
> Why do you wander
> About the streets
> Of the great city
> Of London?
> Why do you start and wince
> When white folk stare at you?
> Don't you think they wonder
> Why a little brown girl
> Should roam about their city
> Their white, white city?
>
> **Una Marson** *The Moth and the Star* 1937

Although the period after the Second World War, with the arrival of the ship *Empire Windrush* in 1948, has become etched in people's minds as the beginning of Caribbean immigration to Britain, in fact it goes back at least a couple of centuries before then. In the eighteenth century, for example, when there were about 10,000 black people in Britain, many of them came from the West Indies. Most were seamen or dock workers in ports such as Liverpool, Bristol and London, though black people lived all over the British Isles, for example in villages in Yorkshire, Devon and Dorset. Some were slave-servants employed to work in large mansions and some became beggars, such as the successful Charles M'Gee. He was born in Jamaica in 1744, known as 'Massa Piebald', and was a regular at his pitch at the bottom of Ludgate Hill, where thousands of people passed him every day. He is described as wearing 'a smart coat': 'He has lost an eye, and his woolly hair, which is almost white, is tied up behind in a tail, with a large tuft at the end, horizontally resting upon the cape of his coat.'

The status of slaves in Britain was legally ambiguous. There was no law against slavery, but neither was there a law permitting it. In 1569 in a case against a man who brought a slave from Russia 'it was resolved, That *England* was too pure an Air for Slaves to breathe in'. Also in 1708 Lord Holt, the Lord Chief Justice, stated that 'as soon as a negro comes into England, he becomes free'. But this view was something of a myth, as Michael Bundock explains: 'There were people in England who were compelled to remain in unfree service which was lifelong and

Charles M'Gee (b. 1744)

unpaid, and with the possibility of being transferred from one master to another.'

This reality was apparent in the announcements offering rewards for the return of runaway slaves, such as the one in the *London Gazette* in 1694: 'A black boy, an Indian, about thirteen years old runaway the 8th inst. from Putney, with a collar about his neck with this inscription: "My Lady Bromfield's black, in Lincoln's Inn Fields." Whoever brings him to Sir Edward Bromfield's at Putney, shall have a guinea reward.'

It was also clear from the many 'For sale' advertisements which appeared in the newspapers, like the one in the *London Advertiser* in 1756: 'To be sold, a Negro Boy, about fourteen years old, warranted free from any distemper, and has had those fatal to that colour: has been used two years to all kinds of household work, and to wait at table; his price is £25.' In 1792 a Bristol citizen sold a black woman for £80 in Jamaican currency and she was transported to Jamaica. Someone who saw her put onboard the ship said that 'her tears flowed down her face like a shower of rain'.

SLAVES AND SERVANTS

'All slaves want to be free – to be free is very sweet.'

Mary Prince *The History of Mary Prince, a West Indian Slave, Related by Herself* 1831

for I am John Edmonstone,
whose name is little known
to evolution's white ladder.
But Darwin will remember me,
just say the black man who taught him
Egypt's ancient art of taxidermy.

John Agard *The Ascent of John Edmonstone* 2009

On the whole these West Indian immigrant slaves were largely anonymous, but some achieved considerable fame. **Francis Barber** (c.1742-1801) for example, became famous as the servant of Dr Samuel Johnson, who was the most celebrated literary figure of the eighteenth century, particularly for his feat in compiling the first English dictionary. This was completed in 1755 after nine years work and it included 113,000 quotations to illustrate the meanings of the 42,773 entries. Dr Johnson was fervently opposed to slavery and referred to Jamaica as a 'den of tyrants, and a dungeon of slaves'. James Boswell records in *The Life of Johnson* (1791), 'Upon one occasion, when in company with some very grave men at Oxford, his toast was "Here's to the next insurrection of the negroes in the West Indies".'

Francis Barber came to England from Jamaica in about 1750, when he was seven or eight years old, as the slave of Colonel Bathurst who had sold his sugar plantation of 2,600 acres along with 143 slaves. He was sent to school in Yorkshire for two years and then returned to London to stay with the Colonel's son, Dr Richard Bathurst, who was a friend of Dr Johnson's. Dr Bathurst then gave Barber to Johnson as a servant. Before Colonel Bathurst died he made a will, in April 1754, declaring: 'I give to Francis Barber a Negroe whom I brought from Jamaica aforesaid into England his freedom.'

Francis Barber (c. 1742-1801) portrait attributed to James Northcote

Barber left Johnson's service for a couple of years to work for an apothecary and he also went to sea. After two years in the Royal Navy he returned to Dr Johnson's household. In 1773 he married a white woman Elizabeth Ball with whom he had four children. In Johnson's last years Barber nursed him in his illness and when Johnson died in 1784 he left Barber an annuity of £70 a year (over £10,000 in today's money) and also the bulk of his estate (now worth about £230,000). In *The Life of Samuel Johnson* Boswell mentions Francis Barber on numerous occasions, referring to him as 'good', 'honest' and 'faithful'.

After Johnson's death Barber and his family moved to Lichfield, Johnson's birth-place. He set up a school, but it was not very successful. In 1801 he died and was buried in the churchyard of St Mary's Church in Stafford. He left behind his widow, two daughters Elizabeth and Ann, and a son Samuel. Samuel eventually became a Methodist preacher in the Potteries and some of his descendants are now in the seventh generation and still living in Staffordshire.

Dennis Barber (a sixth-generation descendant born in 1930) was fascinated by his ancestor, but says that when he was young the matter was frowned upon when it was raised: 'My mother always used to turn round and say, "Look, don't talk about that Black man in front of the children."' His cousin Cedric, born in 1948, found the discovery a positive experience, 'My "black roots" have risen to the forefront of my consciousness in recent years, and I have to say that this awareness of my family revolutionised my life.'

In his biography of Francis Barber (2015), Michael Bundock sums up the bond between Barber and

Johnson: 'It was in many ways a father-son relationship, with all that encompasses in terms of intimacy, possessiveness, exasperation, and love. Johnson had an authoritarian side to his character, yet for the most part he treated Barber with respect and affection, providing him with a home, an education, and the means to live once he was gone. Barber regarded Johnson with honour, giving him support and companionship in the darkest of his often very dark days.'

A contemporary of Francis Barber was **Jonathan Strong** (c.1748-1773) who was influential because of a famous court case. Strong was a slave in Barbados and had been brought to England by his master David Lisle who repeatedly abused him physically. One day he was beaten about the head with a pistol and turned out into the street. He found his way to a surgeon William Sharp who gave free medical advice and treatment to the poor. After Strong was healed, his owner sold him for £30 to a Jamaican planter James Kerr who planned to take him back to the West Indies.

Sharp's brother was the famous Granville Sharp who, along with Thomas Clarkson, was the main campaigner for the abolition of the Slave Trade. The case of Jonathan Strong influenced Granville Sharp to learn about the law and he used his new-found knowledge in order to prevent Strong from being taken back to the Caribbean. This was the first of many cases which Sharp took up to protect the interests of slaves.

In 1772 Lord Justice Mansfield was called upon to make a judgment in the case of the slave James Somerset, whose master wanted to take him back to

Granville Sharp (1735-1813) rescuing a slave from the hands of his master

Virginia. Mansfield delayed his decision several times, saying: 'We are assured that there are no less than 15,000 slaves now in England who will procure liberty, should the law decide in their favour, and whose loss to the proprietary, estimated at a moderate computation, will amount to no less a sum than £700,000.' Eventually, however, he ruled that there was no positive law approving slavery in England, so Somerset could not forcibly be sent abroad. Even then, there was no positive law forbidding slavery.

Nevertheless the judgment was interpreted as a victory for the anti-slavery movement, particularly by London's black community. The following day, for example, the *Middlesex Journal* recorded that 'a great number of Blacks were in Westminster-Hall to hear the determination of the cause and went away greatly pleased'. A few days later the *London Packet* reported that 'near 200 Blacks, with their ladies', gathered 'at a public house in Westminster, to celebrate the triumph which their brother Somerset had obtained over Mr. Stuart his master. Lord Mansfield's health was echoed round the room, and the evening was concluded with a ball. The tickets for admittance to this black assembly were 5s each.'

Mary Prince was famous as the first black woman in Britain to be the subject of a biographical narrative. She was born around 1788 as a slave in Bermuda and also lived in Turks Island and in Antigua before being brought to England in 1828 by her master John Wood and his wife whom she worked for without wages.

Believing she was free in Britain, and after continued ill treatment by the Woods, Prince left their house and found work, first as a charwoman and then as a domestic servant in the household of Thomas Pringle, secretary of the Anti-Slavery Society, and his wife Martha. They tried to buy her freedom, so that she could return to her husband Daniel James, who was a carpenter and a free black man living in Antigua, but John Wood refused to sell her. The Anti-Slavery Society petitioned Parliament on her behalf, on 24 June 1829, expressing 'her desire to return to the West Indies, but not as a slave', but with no success.

In 1831 Pringle arranged for the publication of *The History of Mary Prince, a West Indian Slave, Related by Herself*, which went through three editions in its first year. Prince had told her story to Susanna Strickland who wrote it down and then it was edited by Pringle, so it was a collaborative work.

The autobiography of Mary Prince (1788-c. 1833)

The last paragraph in the book, however, is described as being 'given as nearly as possible in Mary's precise words' and refutes the pro-slavery notion that 'slaves are happy': 'How can slaves be happy when they have the halter round their neck and the whip upon their back? and are disgraced and thought no more of than beasts? – and are separated from their mothers, and husbands, and children, and sisters, just as cattle are sold and separated? Is it happiness for a driver in the field to take down his wife or sister or child, and strip them, and whip them in such a disgraceful manner? – women that have had children exposed in the open field to shame!'

In her preface to the 1987 publication of *The History of Mary Prince*, Ziggi Alexander writes: 'Her story is of interest because she highlights not only the suffering and indignities of enslavement but also the triumphs of the human spirit. She demonstrates how a woman can be enslaved and yet not be a slave. She shows how self-reliance and collective action can transform the individual from passive slave to rebel despite the high costs of freedom, not least of which were physical disabilities, poverty and displacement.' And in *Before Windrush* (2008) Michelle Taylor adds: 'Even though there is no record of Prince after 1833, her text and her work remain as tangible markers of the myriad ways in which the diasporic presence shaped the Empire, well before *Windrush*.'

At the same time that Mary Prince was fighting for her freedom, another slave arrived in Britain, from Guyana. **John Edmonstone**, who was born about 1800, was brought to Glasgow by his master Charles Edmonstone and became free. In Guyana he had been taught how to stuff animals by the Yorkshire eccentric naturalist and explorer Charles Waterton who owned land in the country.

When John Edmonstone moved to Edinburgh in 1823 he worked as a freelance taxidermist mounting specimens for the university's natural history museum. He also lived in the same street as Charles Darwin, who in 1826, at the age of seventeen, was studying medicine at the university, and the two became acquainted. They became friends and Edmonstone started teaching Darwin taxidermy, as he recalls, 'I am going to learn to stuff birds, from a blackamoor I believe an old servant of Dr. Duncan: it has the

Charles Darwin (1809-1882) portrait by George Richmond, 1840

recommendation of cheapness, if it has nothing else, as he only charges one guinea, for an hour every day for two months.'

Darwin also learnt about Guyana and the tropical rain forests and this encouraged him to dream about travelling to South America. He records in his autobiography that Edmonstone 'gained his livelihood by stuffing birds, which he did excellently: he gave me lessons for payment, and I often used to sit with him, for he was a very pleasant and intelligent man'. In *Descent of Man* Darwin discusses the inhabitants of Tierra del Fuego. He refers to Edmonstone when commenting on their intelligence and 'how similar their minds were to ours; so it was with a full-blooded negro with whom I happened once to be intimate'.

During his famous voyage on the *Beagle* (1831-1836) Darwin used Edmonstone's methods for preserving vertebrate specimens and so he can be seen as one of the influences on Darwin's development of his theory of evolution. In *Darwin in Scotland* J. F. Derry concludes that Edmonstone 'played a vital role in giving Darwin ideas of travel, perhaps a new-found maturity, and the means to amass the body of evidence that contributed to his conclusions'.

Fanny Eaton was born (Fanny Antwistle) in the parish of St Andrew, Jamaica, on 23 June 1835. Her mother, formerly a slave, was Matilda Foster, and her father was white, probably an estate owner or manager. Fanny arrived in London with her mother in the 1840s. Matilda worked as a laundress and Fanny as a 'charwoman' or daily cleaner. The 1861 Census records Fanny living with James Eaton, a horse cab proprietor and driver, who was born in 1838 in

Portrait of Fanny Eaton (1835-1924) by Walter Fryer Stocks, 1859

Shoreditch. No record has yet been found that they were married. The couple lived in a small house just south of King's Cross and they eventually had ten children, 6 daughters and 4 sons.

Her claim to fame is based on the fact that she also worked part-time as an artist's model. In the 1860s she was employed by the Royal Academy for their life classes and was paid 5 shillings a session (the equivalent of £12 today). Eaton was painted by famous pre-Raphaelites such as Rossetti and Millais, and also by female artists such as Joanna Boyce

Portrait of Fanny Eaton (1835-1924) by Simeon Solomon, 1859

Wells. In 1865 Rossetti described her in a letter to fellow artist Ford Madox Brown, written when Eaton was thirty, as having 'a very fine head and figure'. The image of her which looks most like her portrait is a chalk sketch on paper by Walter Fryer Stocks. Paintings of her are now on view in the world's greatest art galleries, in guises such as Palestinian, Indian, Hebrew, Egyptian or Libyan, but, as Kathryn Hughes writes (*The Guardian* 12 October 2019): 'The one thing she was never permitted to be was mixed-race Jamaican.'

On 17 February 1881 James Eaton died from a combination of skin rash and blood poisoning (erysipelas pyaemia). At this time Fanny was living in Kensington with seven of her children, from James aged 24 to Frank aged 2, and was working as a needlewoman. By 1891 she was living in Hammersmith, west London, as a 'housekeeper lodger', the lodger being a tailor from Oxford who later married her daughter Mildred

Ten years later she was working as a domestic cook for a wine merchant's family in Oakfield on the Isle of Wight. Two of her daughters had followed her by becoming seamstresses, two were servants and one, Miriam, was briefly a sculptor's assistant before marrying a wool merchant. Miriam has a descendant who remembers Fanny's role as a model being mentioned. Another descendant, who is trying to find out more about his celebrated ancestor, is Brian Eaton, grandson of Fanny's youngest child Frank.

Fanny Matilda Eaton Sexton (b. 1858), Fanny's eldest daughter, from a family photograph, c. 1920

By 1911 Eaton was living with one of her daughters, Julia Powell, her husband and two children, in Hammersmith. She died from unconsciousness due to low blood pressure (senility and syncope) on 4 March 1924, aged 88, and is buried in Margravine Cemetery, Hammersmith. This is the brief, but remarkable, story of a Jamaican immigrant who worked all her life in England as a servant and much of the time also as a single mother.

Dare to Dream the Dream
Asher

There once was a woman
Who dared to dream the dream
There she goes, rocking to an fro
On the boat that would bring her to England

She wash
She cook
She clean
She iron
She standing by she children an she man

An every mickle must make a muckle in her hand
As she scrapes togedda to buy de piece a yam
She remembers how it used to grow in abundance
In her home land

She coulda never buy nuttin expensive
But with her skill create something out of nothing
If only to show her children
How to make the most of a little thing

The dream she had then has faded
Like a bubble disappearing from her hand
But she wants a better future for her children
And she also wants to reach the promised land.

NURSES AND DOCTORS

'When the British Government brought over some skilled technicians from Jamaica at the beginning of the war and placed them in factories in Britain, their English fellow-workers were quite astonished to see them wearing clothes like themselves, were still more surprised when they heard them speak fluent English and were almost paralysed with shock when they saw them working the machines with efficiency and full control.'

Harold Moody *The Colour Bar* 1944

The fame of the Caribbean nurses who migrated to Britain in the 1950s and 60s is now well established. They came to support the new National Health Service which had been established by the Labour Government in 1948. Between 1948 and 1958 the medical workforce in England increased by 30% and in that time around 6,000 women from the Caribbean had arrived to train as nurses in British hospitals. By 1966 the number had doubled. David Lammy, MP for Tottenham, whose parents came from Guyana, writes in *Mother Country*: 'The thousands of nurses and health workers who came to Britain before 1973 formed the backbone of the NHS. They worked with unparalleled pride and dignity – labouring for all Britain's sick and injured.'

But a hundred years earlier another nurse from the West Indies had travelled to England. This was **Mary Seacole** who, after her travels in Panama, came to England in 1854, determined to help the wounded in the Crimean War. When she was refused an interview, she decided to travel the 3,000 miles to the Crimea at her own expense, taking with her a large stock of medicines. On her arrival she established her 'British Hotel', two miles from Balaclava, and, with the help of two Jamaican cooks, provided healthy food for the soldiers.

Seacole spent much of her time helping wounded soldiers on the battle-field. Known as 'Mother' Seacole, she also cured jaundice, diarrhea, dysentery,

Mary Seacole (1805-1881)

severe inflammation of the chest and many other illnesses. She bandaged up the wounded on both sides of the battle, stitching up wounds and split ears, often while the guns were still firing all around her.

After the war ended in March 1856, she returned to England. The following year she published her book *Wonderful Adventures of Mrs Seacole in Many Lands* and four nights of benefit performances were held for her at the Royal Surrey Gardens, a music hall set in park grounds which could hold 10,000 people. It was packed each night, as eleven military bands turned up to play for her.

The Times of Tuesday 28 July 1857 described the event: 'Few names were more familiar to the public

Mary Seacole's book, published in 1857

during the late war that that of Mrs Seacole. At the end of both the first and second parts the name of Mrs Seacole was shouted by a thousand voices. The genial old lady rose from her place and smiled benignantly on the assembled multitude, amid a tremendous and continued cheering. Never did woman seem happier, and never was hearty and kindly greeting bestowed upon a worthier object.'

Mary Seacole lived during the height of the British Empire and Edwards and Dabydeen comment on her imperialist ideology, 'her narrowly patriotic and romantic glorification of war': 'Seacole's patriotism and her attitude to race reveal a split personality. On the one hand, she is sensitive to a black ancestry and sensitive to the racism directed against blacks. On the other, she shows contempt for blacks and non-British peoples, and is eager to declare her half-whiteness.'

She lived to an old age and continued to be recognised in the streets of London by soldiers she had helped in the Crimea. On 14 May 1881 Mary Seacole died and memory of her gradually faded. Not until 1973 did she make the news again, when a group of Jamaican women in London organised the re-consecration of her grave in the Catholic cemetery in Kensal Rise, London. On 14 May 1981 a memorial service was held to mark the centenary of her death and in 1984 her autobiography was reprinted. Finally on 30 June 2016 a statue of her was unveiled in the gardens of St Thomas's Hospital overlooking the Houses of Parliament.

In the year that Mary Seacole died, another West Indian nurse, **Annie Brewster**, took her place in London, appointed as a probationer at the London Hospital in Whitechapel in December 1881. Although the public memory of Seacole's exploits was fading, there were obituaries in the *Manchester Guardian* and *The Times* which wrote that she 'greatly distinguished herself as a nurse on the battlefield and in hospitals during the Crimean War', so it is possible that Brewster was inspired by her famous predecessor.

Annie Brewster's father, Pharour Chaderon Brewster, was a merchant who was born in Barbados, but Annie, her sister Laura and their mother were born in St Vincent. By 1879 her father was a widower living in East Dulwich, south London where he married an English woman Angelina Impey. In 1893 Pharour

Annie Brewster (1858-1902)

moved to the USA, settling in New York, and he died in 1920, aged 85.

Annie was recruited to the London Hospital by the matron Eva Luckes and in 1884 she was appointed to the nursing staff. In 1888 she was promoted to be in charge of the Ophthalmic Wards, dealing especially with old people who were losing their sight, and became known as Nurse Ophthalmic. The matron highly recommended her: 'Annie Brewster was a thoroughly satisfactory probationer, quick, thorough, intelligent and active. She was a favourite with all the sisters under whom she worked. She was equally well

Annie Brewster with the nursing staff at the London Hospital

fitted for medical and surgical work and I was glad to accede to her request to be appointed staff nurse in Women's Medical wards. She was gentle and kind to her patients and showed a good "head" for managing her ward.'

On 8th February 1902 the Ward Report for that week recorded: 'Nurse Ophthalmic was operated on on Friday. A large fibroid was found and removed. So far Nurse is doing very well. It was a relief to know the growth was not malignant.' Tragically the following week, despite everything possible being done for her by Dr Herman, her death was recorded: 'Poor Nurse Ophthalmic who seemed to be getting on so well after her operation (though it was a very big one) got suddenly worse on Tuesday morning, and died quite unexpectedly. There was slight peritonitis but it was difficult to decide what was the actual cause of death.'

Eva Luckes recorded Brewster's '20 years' faithful and devoted service' and wrote her obituary: 'Annie Brewster, best known to all her Hospital friends as

"Nurse O", spent the best and happiest years of her life at the London Hospital. She was with us for just over 20 years – nearly 14 of which had been spent as nurse in charge of the Ophthalmic Wards. With her quick intelligence she became very skilful in the treatment of "eyes" and her kindness to the poor old people who passed through her hands during this period was unwearied. Her health was failing for some time before the end. A serious operation became necessary, and she died in "Mayer Ward" three days afterwards, leaving many Hospital friends to mourn her loss, and to keep her in affectionate remembrance. She was buried by the Hospital at Ilford Cemetery.' The place where she is buried is the City of London Cemetery, Aldersbrook, in the London Borough of Newham.

A number of West Indian immigrants also became famous as doctors, for example Gunn Munro from Grenada, Ferdinand Wright and James Jackson Brown from Jamaica, Roland Cumberbatch from Barbados, George Alfred Busby from Trinidad and Risien Russell from Guyana. As there were no facilities in the Caribbean for medical training, an aspiring doctor had to come to Britain. One of the first was **John Alcindor** who was born in Port of Spain, Trinidad, in 1873. In 1892 he won an Island Scholarship to study 'at some university or other scientific educational institution in the British empire'. He chose to go to Scotland and registered as a student of medicine at Edinburgh University on a course to last a minimum of five years. There were other medical students there at the time, for example from Guyana, St Kitts and Trinidad.

John Alcindor (1873-1924) playing cricket in Paddington

Alcindor graduated in 1899 and moved to London where he worked in a number of hospitals, including Plaistow, Hampstead and Camberwell, before establishing his own medical practice in Paddington. He participated in the Pan-African Conference of July 1900 and in 1911 married Minnie Martin, a journalist and daughter of a Frenchman, who was consequently cut off from her family. They had three sons.

Alcindor was a keen cricketer, described as an 'excellent wicket-keeper and a consistent batsman'. He was a member of the British Medical Association and was the author of several medical publications on subjects such as influenza, cancer and tuberculosis. As a doctor amongst the poor, he realised that many illnesses were caused by poor diet and lack of food. He sometimes went off with the family dinner, saying, 'My patient needs feeding, not doctoring.'

In 1917 he volunteered for the First World War, but was turned down because he was of 'colonial origin'. The following year he joined the Red Cross, serving two nights a week, and was awarded the 1914-18 war medal for the considerable time he spent meeting trainloads of wounded soldiers in London. In 1921 Alcindor became president of a London-based association, the African Progress Union, which gave guidance to students and protested against bigotry in business, politics and the press. The committee included his wife, Edith Barbour-James from Barbados and her friend Agatha Acham Chen form Trinidad. He also took a leading part in the Pan-African congresses of 1921 and 1923.

John Alcindor died in St Mary's Hospital, Paddington, in 1924. The local paper recorded that he had 'a considerable practice among the poor of the Harrow Road neighbourhood and was very popular' and spoke of him as a 'familiar figure in the neighbourhood, a man of colour, and widely known as the "Black Doctor". He was both modest and unassuming in his bearing; also of kindly and sympathetic disposition.' *West Africa* reported: 'Dr. Alcindor was perhaps the best known practitioner in London amongst African people, though his professional skill was by no means limited to them.' After his death his widow ran residential accommodation for Africans in London.

In an article on Alcindor, Jeffrey Green sums up his personal legacy: 'As a family man, he would have been proud of the record of his three sons in the 1939-1945 war and that Cyril, a regular soldier, was an officer in 1944. His three grand-children – a legal secretary, a scientist in space projects and an electrical engineer – have useful and respected positions in modern Britain.'

The most famous doctor from the Caribbean in the first half of the twentieth century was **Harold Moody** who was born in Jamaica in 1882, the son of a pharmacist whose father was white. He came to London in 1904 to study medicine at King's College

When he arrived he discovered the colour bar operating in the country. He found it hard to get lodgings and was denied a hospital appointment because the matron 'refused to have a coloured doctor working at the hospital'. In 1913 he started his own practice in Peckham and eventually made a success of it. In the same year he married a white woman, Olive Tranter, who was a nurse he had met while

Harold Moody (1882-1947)

working on the wards of the Royal Eye Hospital and with whom he was to have six children.

Moody was a Congregationalist lay preacher and a pacifist. His favourite text was from Paul's epistle to the Galatians: 'There is neither Jew nor Greek, there is neither bond nor free, there is neither male nor female: for ye are all one in Christ Jesus.' In 1931 he founded the League of Coloured Peoples, with members of the executive largely from the Caribbean. Among the organisation's aims were 'to promote and protect the

Social, Educational, Economic and Political interests of its members; to interest members in the Welfare of Coloured Peoples in all parts of the World; and to improve relations between the races'.

In 1933 the League started publishing its quarterly magazine *The Keys*, whose one object was 'to improve relations between the Races'. In July of that year it reported the story of a nurse who applied to twenty-five hospitals and found herself refused by every one on the grounds of 'colour'. One of the editors of *The Keys* was Una Marson, who had lodged with Moody when she first arrived from Jamaica, and C. L. R. James also contributed to the journal. The League supported the black seamen in Cardiff, who were virtually all made redundant in 1935, and also the workers demonstrating in the Trinidad oilfields in 1937. The following year Moody had three letters published in *The Times* criticising police brutality against strikers in Jamaica.

Moody's philanthropic work extended to all children born into Britain's black community. Each year he took coach-loads of the youngsters on a summer trip to Epsom and each year he organised a Christmas party for them. He was also concerned about their education and did a survey entitled 'Race Relations and the School' which included groundbreaking recommendations on the training of teachers, classroom practice and the content of text-books, for instance challenging the Eurocentric treatment of Africa – issues which were not really addressed for decades.

During the Second World War Moody shouldered his full share of civil defence work in Peckham. He was called to the New Cross rocket explosion in which nearly 200 were killed and hundreds injured. He often worked night and day amid the falling bombs. He also successfully fought for the right of black servicemen and women to hold commissions in the British armed forces. His children Arundel, Ronald, Garth, Harold and Christine all received army or RAF commissions, the latter two as doctors, and Arundel and Harold both rose to the rank of major.

After the war he was concerned about the plight of mixed-race war babies who needed a home and others whose mothers were in dire need of financial assistance. The League attempted to run its own home for a few children, but illness in the home led to its closure. After a trip to the West Indies and the United States in the winter of 1946-7, Moody died of acute influenza in 1947.

Peter Fryer sums up his contribution: 'Precise and lucid in his writings and speeches, passionate in his emotions but controlled in their expression, tireless in his devotion to his life's work, Moody was thought too cautious, patient and conservative by the younger generation of radicals.' But he adds, 'For all that, he was nobody's Uncle Tom; in his own way he struck blow after well-aimed blow in the struggle against racism.' In 2019 a commemorative plaque was put up at the YMCA in central London.

Stolen Identity
Asher

You go over to Africa
You take away the people house and land
Distressing future generations
What was it about our race
The price which we've paid
For many of us cannot speak
Our original language

You have a reputation
For going to different lands
Marking out your plans
Even having the audacity
To put up your own flags

Check out places like Jamaica
It has names like Maryland
Cornwall, Sheffield and Leeds
Evidence to me of how we have been deceived
Since no one dare to mention
Our emperors, kings and queens

And if that's not bad enough
You tried to exclude us from your books
By putting Florence Nightingale
But no Mary Seacole

We will continue
To explore this history
That which was hidden from us for centuries
It will be seen as a positive way
Of finding our stolen identity
Not to be used for supremacy
But so that we can be proud of our history.

POLITICAL ACTIVISTS

'I am a West-Indian, a lover of liberty, and would dishonour human nature if I did not shew myself a friend to the liberty of others.'

    Robert Wedderburn *The Axe Laid to the Root* 1817

'Emancipate yourself from mental slavery, none but ourselves can free our minds.

    Marcus Garvey October 1937

'War is an essential part of capitalism and can only be abolished by changing the present social system.'

    George Padmore *Africa and World Peace* 1937

I am black,
And so I must be
More clever than white folk
More wise than white folk
More discreet than white folk,
More courageous than white folk.

    Una Marson *Black Burden* 1945

At the beginning of the nineteenth century there were two famous West Indian political activists in England, both mixed-race: one was hanged and decapitated for treason, the other imprisoned for his radical preaching.

William Davidson was born in Kingston, Jamaica, in 1786. At the age of fourteen he was sent to Edinburgh to complete his education and eventually ended up in London where he worked as a cabinet-maker and also taught in a Wesleyan Sunday school in Walworth. He married Mrs Sarah Lane, a poor widow with four sons, and had two more sons with her. Davidson was a popular man with dark eyes and dark curly hair, who invited his neighbours to his birthday party and entertained them with wine and radical songs.

It was a time of great poverty and Davidson held political meetings in his own house, as well as attending many of the large open-air meetings of protest against the repressive government. At one of these meetings he helped guard the banner from capture by the police. It was a black flag with skull and crossbones and read: 'Let us die like Men and not be sold like Slaves'.

The revolutionary group which Davidson belonged to met in Cato Street, off the Edgware Road, where they kept their store of home-made grenades, muskets, pistols, swords and pikes. Davidson was posted as a guard, but they had already been betrayed by a spy and the police stormed the loft and

William Davidson (1786-1820) drawn from life by A. Wivell

overpowered him. He was led away, 'damning every Person that would not die in liberty's cause' and singing 'Scots wha hae wi' Wallace bled'.

At his trial Davidson pleaded not guilty of high treason and told the court, 'My house has been searched and nearly pulled down and not the slightest evidence was found to show I have been guilty of any conspiracy.' He referred to Magna Carta and defended the English tradition of resisting tyranny. Then he said, 'I have no objection to tender my life in the service of my country, but let me at least, for the sake of my children, save my character from the disgrace of dying a traitor. For my children only do I feel, and when I think of them I am deprived of utterance – I can say no more.'

On 1 May 1820, along with his four white comrades, Davidson died bravely on the scaffold outside

Newgate Jail in front of the largest crowd ever to turn out for an execution. The authorities were so concerned at the enormous crowd and the sympathies of the people for the prisoners that a civil force of 700 men stood by to keep order and to prevent any attempt at rescuing the five men. Artillery had been drawn up and horse guards patrolled the streets.

Davidson climbed the scaffold with a firm step, bowed to the crowd and said his prayers while clasping the hand of the attending clergyman. His last words were, 'God bless you all! Good-bye.' The crowd booed and hissed, shouting 'Murder!' and 'Bring out the spy, Edwards. Hang him!' After Davidson was hanged and beheaded, his widow begged King George III to be allowed to take away the mutilated remains of her husband for a decent burial, but he refused her request and the body was buried in quicklime in Newgate Jail.

The famous radical journalist Richard Carlile, in prison for fighting for the freedom of the press, sent Mrs Davidson £2 and asked others to help her too. He wrote to her: 'Be assured that the heroic manner in which your husband and his companions met their fate, will in a few years, perhaps in a few months, stamp their names as patriots, and men who had nothing but their country's weal at heart. I flatter myself as your children grow up, they will find that the fate of their father will rather procure them respect and admiration than its reverse.'

A few years before Davidson was hanged **Robert Wedderburn** produced a number of periodicals entitled *The Axe Laid to the Root or A Fatal Blow to Oppressors* which contained articles on religion and politics, reviews and poems about slavery. Wedderburn linked the struggle against oppression in Britain to the fight against slavery in the West Indies. He predicted that 'the island of Jamaica will be in the hands of the blacks within twenty years. Prepare for flight, ye planters, for the fate of St. Domingo awaits you.'

Wedderburn was born in Jamaica 'about the year 1762' of a Scottish father and Jamaican mother. He knew about slavery – his grandmother had been flogged almost to death and his mother had been raped by his slave-owning father. At the age of sixteen he went to sea, ending up in England, where he became a tailor. He eventually joined a radical political group called the Spenceans, who believed in equality and restoring the land to the people.

Wedderburn became famous for the revolutionary rhetoric with which he entertained the crowds at Hopkins Street chapel, which was a converted hayloft in Soho. Government spies regularly attended the meetings and in 1819 one spy reported: 'The sense of the meeting was taken,- Question "has a Slave an inherent right to slay his master who refuses him his Liberty." Nearly the whole of the persons in the room held up their hand in favour of the Question. Mr W. then exclaimed, well Gentlemen I can *now write home and tell the Slaves to murder their Masters as soon as they please.*'

The Home Secretary called Wedderburn a 'notorious firebrand' and his oratory was so powerful that he was put on the Government's secret list of 33 leading reformers. He was accused of sedition, but acquitted. Then he was re-arrested on a charge of blasphemy and in 1820 was sent to jail for two years.

Robert Wedderburn (1762-1835)

When he came out, he continued his revolutionary activity and in 1824 he published his own autobiography entitled *The Horrors of Slavery*, in which he wrote: 'I am the offspring of a slave, it is true; but I am a man of free thought and opinion; and though I was immured for two years in his Majesty's gaol at Dorchester, for daring to express my sentiments as a free man, I am still the same as I was before, and imprisonment has but confirmed me that I was right. They who know me, will confirm this statement.'

He also explained why he could not return to Jamaica: 'I should have gone back to Jamaica, had I not been fearful of the planters; for such is their hatred of anyone having black blood in his veins, and who dares to think and act as a free man, that they would almost certainly have trumped up some charge against me, and hung me. With them I should have no mercy.'

Wedderburn concludes his account by saying: 'I thank my GOD that through a long life of hardship and adversity, I have ever been free both in mind and body: and I have always raised my voice in behalf of my enslaved countrymen.'

At the end of the nineteenth century two West Indians emerged on to the British political scene, concentrating particularly on the fight for African freedom from colonialism. **Celestine Edwards** was born in Dominica around 1858, the youngest of ten children, and at the age of 12 he stowed away on a French ship and became a seaman. In the 1870s he settled in Edinburgh and later lived in Sunderland, before moving to Hackney in London. Here he worked as a building labourer and made speeches in Victoria Park on such issues as slavery. As a Methodist, he also lectured on temperance and wrote religious pamphlets.

In 1892 Edwards became editor of *Lux*, a 'weekly Christian Evidence Newspaper', and in an editorial on 10 December 1892, he wrote about Britain's seizure of Uganda: 'As long as such unrighteous deeds as cold-blooded murders are permitted under the British flag, as long as avarice and cupidity prompt the actions of a

Portrait of Celestine Edwards (c. 1858-1894), from Lux, 29 July 1893

missionary nation, so long we shall protest against public money being spent in the interest of land-grabbers.' The following year (18 February) he again spoke up for African liberation: 'The day is coming when Africans will speak for themselves. The day is breaking and the despised African, whose only crime is his colour, will yet give an account of himself. We think it no crime for Africans to look with suspicion upon the European who has stolen a part of their country and deluged it with rum and powder, under the cover of civilisation.'

Edwards also compared Muslims favourably with Christians: 'The Mohammedans do try to make the people sober, which is a vast improvement upon our drunken colonies in West Africa. It is true that we pretend to be going for the express purpose of putting down the slave trade, with a kind of righteous indignation and horror at the wickedness of the followers of Islam, when the truth is that we substitute a system which is worse than slavery.'

In 1893 he also published *Fraternity*, the monthly magazine of the Society for the Recognition of the Universal Brotherhood of Man, which reached a circulation of more than 7,000. As well as editing these two papers, Celestine Edwards toured the country, speaking about racism, colonialism and lynching in America. In Newcastle, for example, he told an audience: 'My ancestors proudly trod the sands of the African continent, but from their home and friends were dragged into the slave mart and sold to the planters of the West Indies. The very thought that my race should have been so grievously wronged is almost more than I can bear. Of the condition of my people today I but tarry to say that by diligence, thought and care they have given the lie to many a false prophet who, prior to their Emancipation, sought to convince the world that the black man was in all respects unfit for freedom. Their position today is one over which I proudly rejoice. To their future I look with confidence.'

Edwards worked tirelessly for the cause. He also wanted to become a doctor and enrolled at the London Hospital, but his health was poor and in May 1894 he returned to his family in the West Indies to try and recover. He died there in his brother's arms on 25 July 1894. An obituary recalled, 'He was proud of his colour and his people. He lived not for himself.'

Another West Indian soon took the place of Celestine Edwards in the political arena. His name is **Henry Sylvester Williams**, born on 19 February 1869 in the village of Arouca in Trinidad. His father had settled there from Barbados and worked as a wheelwright.

Williams qualified as a teacher at the early age of 17 and eventually came to London to study law. In 1897 he founded the African Association, whose aims included 'to encourage a feeling of unity to facilitate friendly intercourse among Africans in general' and to circulate 'accurate information on all subjects affecting their rights'. Sylvester Williams was the Association's secretary and its president was Rev Henry Mason Joseph from Antigua.

The following year Williams got married to a white woman, Agnes Powell, who was a member of the Temperance Society and came from Gillingham in Kent. In the same year he issued a circular calling for

Sylvester Williams (1869-1911)

a world conference of black people, particularly those in 'South Africa, West Africa and the West Indies'. In 1899 he coined the term 'Pan-African' and in 1900 the Pan-African Conference committee, with Williams as chair and Joseph as secretary, organised the first Pan-African conference which took place at Westminster Town Hall in July. Booker T. Washington said it was likely 'to be one of the most effective far-reaching gatherings that has ever been held in connection with the development of the race'. Williams himself wrote that the conference would be the 'first occasion upon which black men would assemble in England to speak for themselves and endeavour to influence public opinion in their favour'.

There were 30 delegates and among the speakers were C. W. French from St Kitts demanding equal rights; John E. Quinlan from St Lucia arguing that capitalists were trying to enslave black people again, especially in South Africa; and William Myer, a Trinidadian medical student, who attacked pseudo-scientific racism for 'trying to prove that negroes were worthless and depraved persons who had no right to live'.

This first Pan-African Association did not last long, but it was to inspire the later Pan-African Congresses which took place in Paris in 1919, organised by W. E. B. du Bois, London in 1921 and 1923, and Manchester in 1945. Also it did produce a journal called *The Pan-African*, launched by Williams in October 1901, which was designed to spread information 'concerning the interests of the African and his descendants in the British Empire'. The editorial of the first issue claimed that 'no other but a Negro can represent the Negro' and that 'the times demand the presence of that Negro to serve the deserving cause of the most despised and ill-used today'.

The journal was short-lived, however, and only about half a dozen issues appeared. Williams became a barrister in 1902, probably the first of African descent to practise in Britain. In 1906 he joined the Fabian Society and won a seat on Marylebone Borough Council as a Progressive and Labour Party candidate. In 1908 he returned to Trinidad with his family and established a successful legal practice in Port-of-Spain. He died of a kidney ailment on 26 March 1911, leaving his wife and five children. She was not very well off and had to take in lodgers, one of whom was H. A. Nurse, George Padmore's father.

In a critical biography of Williams, J. R. Hooker concludes: 'He was certain that black people were the equals of any set of humans; and he could point to a large number, including himself, who already had demonstrated the proposition. He sought justice and fair competition. He was, finally, a decent and generous man.'

The most famous West Indian in the first half of the twentieth century was **Marcus Garvey** who settled in England in 1935 and stayed there for the remainder of his life. He was born in St Ann's Bay, Jamaica, on 17 August 1887. His father was a mason and a deacon in the Methodist Church; his mother a domestic worker and farmer. He had to leave school at the age of fourteen to help support his family.

Garvey went to Kingston to become a printer, which was to help him in his numerous publications. In 1908 he took part in a strike by printers and was fired from his job. The following year his newspaper *The Watchman* began publication, but only lasted for three issues. He first came to England in 1912 where he met black seamen and students and was attracted to the ideals of the Labour Party. He believed in the solidarity of the oppressed and supported Gandhi's anti-colonial struggle in India.

Most of Garvey's life was spent in America where he built up the largest African American mass movement in American history, the Universal Negro Improvement Association, whose aim was 'the general uplift of the Negro people of the world'. He lectured in liberty halls across the United States to audiences of tens of thousands of people, greeted by tumultuous applause. Many of his audience were also British Caribbean immigrants.

As C. L. R. James wrote, 'Garvey organized more American blacks into a politically race-conscious movement than the continent of America had ever seen before or since': 'The impact of Garvey's philosophy, has had, in my opinion, more effect in shaping current beliefs of blacks in their cultural values and in the wisdom of economic development and determination than any other force. When you bear in mind the slenderness of his resources, the vast material forces and the pervading social conceptions which automatically sought to destroy him, Garvey's achievement remains one of the propagandistic miracles of this century.'

In 1918 Garvey founded a weekly newspaper called *Negro World* in which many of his speeches and essays appeared. It enjoyed a circulation of nearly a quarter of a million readers. His 'Back to Africa' slogan

Marcus Garvey (1887-1940)

was aimed at restoring respect for African culture among black Americans and, long before the Civil Rights Movement, he said, 'I shall teach the black man to see beauty in himself.'

He eventually returned to Kingston, where he founded a magazine called the *Black Man* in December 1933. When he travelled to London in 1935 he continued to address large crowds, especially at Speakers' Corner in Hyde Park, and in every issue of his publication he carried on his campaign on behalf of the Ethiopian resistance to Italian occupation. The magazine also contained articles by the Guyanese writer Eric Walrond who had settled in England in 1932. The *Black Man* circulated widely in the USA, the West Indies, Central America and Africa.

Garvey died on 10 June, 1940, aged 52 and was buried in Kensal Green Cemetery. On 15 November, 1964, however, the government of Jamaica proclaimed him Jamaica's first national hero and had his remains brought from England and placed in a shrine in National Heroes Park. Although he died in relative obscurity, he later had a great influence on the Black Power and Civil Rights movements and on Rastafarianism. His memory is kept alive through reggae artists such as Burning Spear, Mighty Diamonds and Bob Marley.

The radical Jamaican activist Richard Hart, who also spent his last years in England, disagreed with Garvey's politics, but praised his enormous political achievement: 'The really progressive element in Garvey's teaching in the USA was that he successfully challenged the imperialist doctrine of Negro inferiority which millions of Negroes in the Western world had themselves come to accept. Though the projected return to Africa never did take place, his efforts were not wasted. Those who had been inspired by Garvey's message now had the self-respect and self-confidence to struggle for their rights and improve their conditions right where they were in the USA and the West Indies.'

Garvey's first wife **Amy Ashwood Garvey**, who helped found the UNIA and was one of its secretaries, was a political activist in her own right. She was born around 1895 in Port Antonio, Jamaica, and met Marcus in 1914. They were married in 1919, but divorced a couple of years later.

According to *The Oxford Companion to Black British History* she was 'not only a political activist, but also a journalist, music producer, playwright, lecturer, and businesswoman'. In 1935 she settled in England where she opened the International Afro Restaurant in London's New Oxford Street and also ran the Florence Mills Social Club (named after the African American night-club entertainer) near Carnaby Street. One of those who played in the club was the celebrated clarinetist and jazz conductor Rudolph Dunbar who came from Guyana and settled in London in 1931.

Tony Martin describes her significance at that time: 'She became a pivotal figure around whom revolved a brilliant coterie of young African and West Indian activists. These were mostly young men who were destined to be among the heirs to the struggle that Garvey had waged so magnificently in the 1920s. These were the men who before long would see that struggle through to political independence in the Pan-African world. The young activists who moved in Amy's circle constitute a veritable who's who of pre-independence African and Caribbean politics.'

Martin mentions, for example, C. L. R. James, George Padmore, Kwame Nkrumah, Jomo Kenyatta and Eric Williams: 'Together they quickly catapulted London into pre-eminence in the world of Pan-African agitation.' He goes on to say, 'Amy was a splendid cook, her food was as reasonably priced as it was excellent and her place soon became the centre of a good deal of West Indian agitation.' C. L. R. James confirms her culinary skills: 'She was very important to me, because from those early days to this day, I find English food uneatable.' He also describes her as a 'militant anti-imperialist', a 'woman of tremendous personality' and 'one of the brightest women I have known'.

The famous West Indian cricketer Learie Constantine used to visit when he was in London and became good friends with Amy. Clare Midgley writes that Amy 'played a crucial role in linking West African activists to West Indians and African-Americans' : 'The Florence Mills Social Parlour in Carnaby Street, which she set up as a social centre for black people in London, formed part of a web of social support sustained by black women which was vital both to cement black political networks and in creating homes-from-home within an alien and racist environment.'

It was in Amy's restaurant that C. L. R. James organised the International African Friends of Abyssinia which he chaired, with Amy as treasurer. She addressed a meeting in Liverpool, attended by 'several hundred of the black community', which discussed sanctions against Italy and the possibility of closing the Suez Canal. In August 1935 she spoke at a

Amy Ashwood Garvey (c. 1895-1969)

rally in Trafalgar Square, organised by the Labour Party, saying, 'No race has been so noble in forgiving, but now the hour has struck for our complete emancipation.'

Amy Ashwood Garvey campaigned widely in Africa and the Caribbean and was still active in England after the war. She chaired the opening day of the Pan-African Congress held in Manchester in October 1945. She lived in Birmingham for a while where she supported black children in schools. When Claudia Jones founded the *West Indian Gazette* Amy joined the editorial board and helped finance it. She also chaired the organisation set up in response to the Notting Hill riots in 1958, contributed to the Kelso Cochrane Fund and supported the black youths who had been arrested. She became president of the Association for the Advancement of Coloured People, with David Pitt as vice-president and Claudia Jones as secretary.

Amy died of cancer in Jamaica in 1969. C. L. R. James placed her among the handful of brilliant conversationalists he had ever met, which included Leon Trotsky and the West Indian cricketer Frank Worrell, 'What I am dealing with here is a unique capacity to concentrate all the forces available and needed for the matter in hand, usually conversation, but, I suspect, applicable in other fields.'

Another West Indian who enjoyed the hospitality of Amy's club and helped to finance it was **T. Ras Makonnen** who said: 'You could go there after you'd been slugging it out for two or three hours at Hyde Park or some other meeting and get a lovely meal, dance and enjoy yourself.'

T. Ras Makonnen (c. 1900-1983)

Makonnen was born George Thomas Nathaniel Griffith in the village of Buxton, Guyana, around 1900. (He changed his name to Makonnen after the Italian invasion of Abyssinia in 1936.) After spending some time in America, he settled in London in 1937 and then moved to Manchester where he established a chain of restaurants and a night-club. His business skills were based on his upbringing in Guyana: 'I think a lot of the success of these ventures could be attributed to the fact that I was no stranger to business. My early orientation in Guyana, the observation I had made of my father in the diamond industry meant that I was prepared to venture where someone with no background would hesitate.'

His aim, however, was not merely financial, but political: 'But I did not regard these restaurants as mine, nor the takings for that matter. This was what the Pan-African thing was all about. I suppose I felt that they made it possible to carry on a whole range of defence operations for blacks at home and abroad.'

His profits enabled Makonnen to set up the Pan-African Publishing Company, whose directors included C. L. R. James and George Padmore, and to open a bookshop called the Economist in Oxford Road, Manchester. In 1937 he helped set up the International African Service Bureau, with Padmore as chair and himself as secretary, to campaign for 'educational and economic assistance for people of African descent worldwide'. They produced a short-lived duplicated paper called *Africa and the World*. Makonnen also

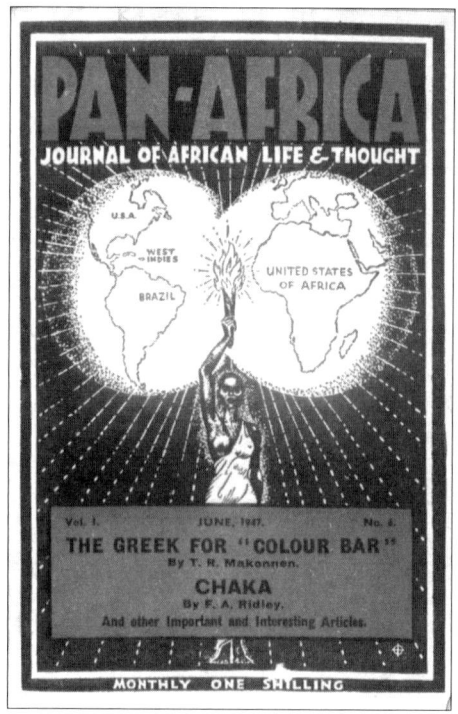

Pan-Africa June 1947

financed a monthly journal *International African Opinion*, edited by C. L. R. James.

He describes how he sold this publication: 'With the paper printed I would then look up the halls where leftist meetings or peace meetings were on that night, and sell this thing illegally at the door on the way out. I would make pounds and pounds this way, because many an old English lady would give me ten shillings just to get rid of me. The other place I sold a large number was after speaking in Hyde Park. So sometimes I would clear more than £20 worth in a single meeting. After paying the printers, there would be still large savings, and I gradually built up capital without the other fellows noticing.'

The journal only lasted a year, partly because of its radical stance. According to Padmore, 'The journal excited alarm in official quarters and was banned by East African colonial governments as "seditious".' It was 'finally forced to close down so as not to jeopardize the liberties of subscribers who were made liable to imprisonment if found reading the magazine'.

Minkah Makalani quotes Makonnen as saying, 'England had been the executioner of its own colonial empire' for it 'allowed these blacks to feel the contrast between freedom in the metropolis and slavery in the colonies'. Makalani goes on to say, 'London served as an incubator, a cauldron whose pressures Makonnen recalled forced black activists "into making alliances across boundaries that would have been unthinkable back home".'

In 1946 Makonnen was told about a Jamaican airman, Donald Beard, who was charged with murder after a fight in Manchester involving 'a group of about

40 West Indian RAF chaps' who had been 'attacked by a group of white boys'. He immediately sought the help of Norman Manley and paid £1,500 to bring him over from Jamaica to defend Beard. The police claimed to have identified the suspect at a distance of fifty yards, but it was snowing heavily that night and Manley was able to prove that visibility had been less than ten yards. The judge dismissed the case saying 'he had never seen such a brilliant performance'.

After the Second World War Makonnen was concerned about the 'hundreds of illegitimate children born of English women' as a 'result of the black American soldiers in Britain', as he notes: 'This confronted all of us with a problem. We tackled it in two ways. Sir Learie Constantine got some help from his Jewish friends in Leeds, and I gave over £5,000 to found a home for coloured children.'

In 1945 Makonnen helped organise the Fifth Pan-African Congress in Manchester and in 1947 founded the monthly periodical *Pan-Africa*. He was the Publishing and Managing Editor. Associate editors included Kenyatta, Nkrumah and H. W. Springer from Barbados. Makonnen emigrated to Ghana in 1957, then to Kenya, where he died in 1983.

A man who shared a flat with Makonnen in London in 1937 was **George Padmore**. C. L. R. James, who was his life-long friend, wrote of him that he was 'the originator of the movement to achieve political independence of the African countries and people of African descent. That is why he is increasingly known as the Father of African emancipation.'

Padmore was born Malcolm Ivan Meredith Nurse in Arouca, Trinidad, in 1902 or 1903, the grandson of an enslaved African. He studied sociology and political science in America and joined the Communist Party in 1927 when he adopted his pseudonym. In 1929 he went to Moscow and was appointed the head of the Soviet Negro Bureau. As editor of the *Negro* Worker in Hamburg in 1931, he is said to have had about 4,000 contacts in various colonial countries. After leaving the Party, owing to disagreements on its policy on imperialism, Padmore settled in London in 1935.

He made a living by private tuition and journalism, often writing for the Independent Labour Party's weekly, the *New Leader*, and other left-wing publications like *Socialist Leader* and *Tribune*. Although he never joined the ILP he became its colonial expert. In 1936 he published *How Britain Rules Africa*, describing the history and current state of Britain's African colonies and explaining that it was necessary that the British public 'should know something of the conditions under which the Blacks live and toil in those territories which constitute the British African Empire': 'Everywhere we shall see stark imperialist oppression and exploitation, allied with racial ignorance and arrogance, swaggering about without the least sign of shame. Such brutality and barbarity remind us of conditions in Germany today.'

The following year he wrote *Africa and World Peace*, in which he recounts how at the Berlin conference, convened by Bismarck in 1885, the European powers carved up the African continent, quoting Gladstone as saying, 'If Germany is to become a colonizing power, all I say is "God speed her."' Padmore predicted Hitler's attack on Czechoslovakia and commented, 'There is as much

Fascist terrorism in India and Africa as would make Mussolini and Hitler blush.'

When Mussolini's troops marched into Abyssinia, Padmore, Amy Ashwood Garvey, C. L. R. James and others formed the International African Friends of Abyssinia to arouse the British public's sympathy and support for the victim of fascist aggression and 'to assist by all means in their power in the maintenance of the Territorial integrity and political independence of Abyssinia'. When the defeated emperor Haile Selassie came to London in 1936 the IAFA arranged a reception for him at Waterloo station.

During the Second World War Padmore organised protests against Churchill's Atlantic Charter which promised that 'sovereign rights and self-government' would be restored to peoples who had lost them, but that this did not apply to British colonies. This was the reason he refused to fight for the British Empire: 'I think it is a piece of bold effrontery to expect a victim of Imperialism, who is excluded from all the lofty declarations of the Atlantic charter, to contribute to the perpetuation of my own enslavement.' At the Pan-African Congress in Manchester he demanded 'complete and absolute independence' for West Africa, equality for all in South Africa, federation and self-government for the British West Indies and that 'discrimination on account of race, creed or colour be made a criminal offence by law'.

George Padmore was Kwame Nkrumah's personal representative in London during the struggle for Ghanaian independence and spent the last two years of his life, up to 1959, as Nkrumah's personal political adviser on Pan-African questions in Ghana. In

George Padmore (c. 1902-1959) in 1937

Caribbean Liberators Jerome Teelucksingh writes of Padmore: 'The forgotten hero of the Caribbean was resilient and determined to build a crusade to liberate countries. He must be credited for having sown the seeds of anti-colonialism and laid the foundation of an indestructible anti-imperialist movement which resulted in the collapse of colonialism and birth of political independence.'

Padmore's name is kept alive by the George Padmore Institute which is an 'archive, educational research and information centre housing materials relating mainly to the black community of Caribbean, African and Asian descent in Britain and continental Europe'. It was set up in 1991 by New Beacon Books, one of Britain's first post-war black publishers, and is located in Stroud Green Road, north London.

A contemporary of Padmore, who brought a different emphasis to the politics of West Indian immigrants, was **Una Marson**, who came to England from Jamaica in 1932. She was already a successful journalist and in 1928 had founded the monthly journal *Cosmopolitan*. She had also published two volumes of poetry. The year she left Jamaica her play *At What a Price* was staged in Kingston to public acclaim. When she arrived in London she soon got involved with The League of Coloured Peoples. She edited a number of issues of *The Keys* and in one she wrote, 'The Negro world must come together. And who is going to do these things for us? We have to do it ourselves.'

Marson soon realised the racism of many of the people she had once looked up to and wrote a damning poem which was published in the first edition of *The Keys*:

Una Marson (1905-1965)

They called me 'Nigger',
Those little white urchins,
They laughed and shouted
As I passed along the street,
They flung at me:
'Nigger! Nigger! Nigger!'
What made me keep my fingers
From choking the words in their throats?
What made my face grow hot,
The blood boil in my veins
And tears spring to my eyes?
What made me go to my room
And sob my heart away
Because white urchins
Called me 'Nigger'?

It is likely that Marcus Garvey read her poem, for he wrote in 1933: 'Our countrywoman Miss Una Marson went to England some time ago to be disillusioned. She thought she was going to a country where she would be accepted on equal terms with those who built it and made its civilization possible. Like most of our race, she thought we have nothing else to do than to project ourselves into the civilization of other people and to claim all its rights. When she found a contrary attitude, she rebelled and wrote some very nasty things about the English.'

Marson developed an interest in Pan-Africanism and in 1934 met the King of Ghana. After the Italian invasion of Ethiopia in 1935 she offered her help to the Ethiopian Minister to London, Charles Martin, and went on to work as personal secretary to Haile Selassie when he fled to England.

Una Marson was the first black woman to be invited to the League of Nations in Geneva and in 1935 she was the Jamaican delegate to an International Women's Conference in Istanbul attended by 300 women from 30 different countries. Her speech was greeted with tumultuous applause and the *Manchester Guardian* reported that this 'negro woman of African origin from the former slave world of Jamaica, brought a new note into the assembly and astonished them by the vigour of her intellect and by her feminist optimism'. According to Delia Jarret-Macauley, 'In the space of three years Una had become the leading black feminist activist in London.' And Alison Donnell adds, 'What is most daring about her contribution was her willingness to break the masculine consensus of the West Indian intellectual community.'

She was still very much concerned with conditions in Jamaica and gave evidence to the Moyne Commission which was investigating the causes of the political disturbances of the 1930s throughout the Caribbean. On a return trip to Jamaica in 1937 she wrote an article in which she said: 'Are we the younger generation to remain resigned to the sham and shallowness of the artificial life into which we have been cast? Are we to remain strangers in our own land, eaters of crumbs that fall from the tables of others when we have it in our power to sit at a table well garnished by our own hands?'

Perhaps her most famous achievement was her work with the BBC where, in 1941, she became a full-time programme assistant for *Calling the West Indies*. This led two years later to her devising the radio programme *Caribbean Voices* which launched the

Una Marson broadcasting from London on the BBC

careers of numerous Caribbean authors, including Derek Walcott, George Lamming and Sam Selvon. The Barbadian poet Edward Kamau Brathwaite called the programme 'the single most important literary catalyst for Caribbean creative and critical writing in English'. Marson continued to produce the programme until 1945 when she returned to Jamaica, where she was greeted by huge crowds. In 1949 she became the organising secretary for the Pioneer Press, Jamaica's first serious publishing house, which was the first to publish work by Louise Bennett.

Alison Donnell sums up Una Marson's achievements: 'She was a woman of extraordinary creativity and ambition, qualities which she directed towards the great causes of her time: the advancement of women's rights; the struggle against colonialism; and the strengthening of cultural and literary nationalism.'

Raise Up The Low
Asher

Raise up the low
Bring down the mighty
That's what we do
To bring about equality
We line up we self
Wid all man like Shelley
For they are few
And we are many, many...

Many a work
And see none
A de money

Children work
In sweat shops
Yet dem walk
De streets scruffy

You want de work do
No want to see your
Hands dirty

Toilet cleaning
Sweeping streets
You find dat too lowly

Employ de immigrants
And pay dem lousy
When you look now
You done turn dem
Into enemy

Racists a say
Dem taking over de country
We know they're making you
A whole heap a money

Me say
Raise up the low...

Member when dem use to
Say de same ting to we
Are you a monkey?
Do you swing from trees?

No blacks
No dogs
No Irish
If you please
And what you doing here?
Go back to your country

Me say sambo and nigga
Was a few names for we
You rarely saw a black face
On the TV

You were taking a risk
When you went out a street

Beaten by the public
Beaten by the police

Dem would say
You was dunce
An you really can't read
At de bottom a de barrel
Is where dem had we

Now you're sat a in a Babylon
Wid flat screen TV
A run off your mouth
Wid selective memory

It's a lack of education
If you know what a mean
If you can't show the immigrant
No sympathy
If you can't align yourself
Wid a shared story
Then you're doing to the immigrants
What Britain did to we

Raise up the low...

The Spoken Word
Asher

I have my foundation
It is here I make my stand
It is solid as a rock
It will not sink into the sand

For de rock where I stand pan
Is de spoken word tradition
An right now me a lift it
To its rightful position

Despite the opposition
Me have me ammunition
Me no want my people tink say
Dat me lost me education

For de spoken word was here
Before we wrote it down on paper
Respect to my ancestors
If I deny myself this truth
Then to myself I am a traitor

So big up
Big up
To the cultural orators

Like Marcus Garvey
Who made me proud of me colour

And Martin Luther King
Left us with words
That we could savour
A caged bird must be free
Respect to Paul Laurence Dunbar

And if you try to diss this style
I know I have the answer
I'll fall back on a proverb
If it means it makes you wiser
I have plenty of tricks
Just like Anansi the spider

So if you want to test me
I will trap you in your corner
Return you to your roots
Like Sojourner Truth.

SOLDIERS AND AIRMEN

'They called me Rear-gunner William Tell, then Rear-gunner David after they asked me where I learned to shoot so straight and I said throwing stones back home. I was their David with my mechanical slingshot finding the temple of the giant every time.'

Fred D'Aguiar *A Jamaican Airman Foresees His Death* 1991

black and proud
but not defined by blackness;
the essential I
resides beneath the skin.

Cy Grant *Identity II* 2008

'Billy Strachan, like many black and working-class political activists, has been sadly neglected and even ignored by both black and white historians of the post-war era. His was a life full of achievement.'

David Horsley *Billy Strachan* 2019

West Indian soldiers have been fighting for the British for over 350 years. In the seventeenth century local militias were established in the Caribbean and in 1795 West Indian troops were formed from among the enslaved populations to fight for Britain during the Napoleonic Wars. Within four years there were 12 such regiments in the British West Indies. They were deployed in the British West African colonies, for example Ghana and Sierra Leone, and also used to suppress rebellions, for instance in Barbados in 1816 and Jamaica in 1865.

Four million non-white non-Europeans fought In the First World War. Hundreds of thousands of Africans died serving the British Empire in Africa, but were buried, unlike those who were white, without a record of their names. The chairman of the Commonwealth War Graves Commission, Winston Churchill, wrote that 'the commission would not erect individual headstones but a central memorial in some suitable locality to be selected by the government concerned'. As David Lammy MP writes (*The Observer* 3 November 2019): 'We can't say that we remember all our war dead with honour and dignity and yet exclude a third of a million people who died in their own country serving Britain.'

Over 15,000 West Indian soldiers also served in World War 1, in nine battalions. Many were labourers, digging trenches, carrying shells and building roads, rather than fighting men, but some saw front-line action in Flanders, Palestine and Jordan. They suffered regular discrimination in pay and conditions. 1,130 Jamaicans died in the war, most from the British West Indies Regiment which had enlisted 10,300 from the island. 16 soldiers from the British West Indies Regiment were decorated for bravery.

One Jamaican who fought on the Western Front was Herbert Morris, who was born in 1900 and volunteered at the age of 16. At the battle of Ypres he suffered severe shell shock and went absent without leave, was caught and then absconded again. He was court-martialed and sentenced to be shot for desertion. Just before his 17th birthday, on 20 September 1917, he was executed at dawn by a firing squad consisting of seven West Indians and three white soldiers.

The most famous Jamaican who fought was **Norman Manley**, born in 1893, who later founded the People's National Party in 1938, became Chief Minister from 1955 to 1959 and Premier from 1959 to 1962. Manley's father, who was partly African and partly English, died when he was six years old and his mother, who was of Irish descent, died when he was 16. At college he held the 100 yards record which lasted 40 years. He also won a Rhodes scholarship to study at Oxford University. He arrived in England in 1914 shortly after the outbreak of war and said he found Oxford a 'ghost-like city', as around 70% of the students had already enlisted. He instantly became aware of the racism in English society: 'It was impossible to be in England and not be aware of the problem of colour. You were immediately aware in a thousand ways that you belonged elsewhere but not there.'

Norman Manley (1893-1969)

In 1915 Norman and his brother Roy joined the army and he was promoted to corporal: 'Here I came up against violent colour prejudice. The rank and file disliked taking advice from a coloured N.C.O. and their attitude was mild by comparison with that of my fellow N.C.O.'s.' The following year he was sent to France where he became a gun-layer: 'I was the fastest gun-layer in the battery. A gun-layer, by the way, is the man who operated a fairly complex unit that sets the gun dead on target when it is fired.' In his autobiography he describes the battle of the Somme where in four months they advanced six miles at a cost of half a million lives.

At the battle of Ypres (which the soldiers called 'Wipers') in June 1917 his brother Roy, who was only 21 years old, was killed. As the Germans attacked Roy ran out carrying on his back a man thought to be wounded, but it turned out he was dead, 'then he too fell, killed by a shell that burst a little distance off and sent a small fragment of its casing straight into his heart'. As Manley recalls, 'I cannot speak of how I felt. We were good friends and I was to be lonely for the rest of the war – lonely and bitter.' He also describes the ferocity of the battle: 'I fired my gun without break for forty-six hours, firing a round a minute for the last twelve hours. Very few gunners survived.' He had two miraculous escapes, one from an exploding shell and another from fragments of a gas shell.

Manley also experienced the horrors of Paschendale which he calls the greatest failure of the war. It lasted 5 months and cost the British 750,000 men killed and wounded. The Germans broke through and advanced 45 miles in 5 days, with Paris only 20 miles away. Manley was lost for 6 days, not knowing where the front line was, some troops advancing and some retreating. The Germans had dropped propaganda leaflets warning black soldiers of special destructive treatment, saying they had no reason to take part in a white man's war, so when it appeared as if the Germans were going to invade their position, Manley recalls: 'I loaded my rifle, the rifle I had thought never to use, with care and prepared to sell my life dearly, not in the cliché sense, but for the practical reason that I was half-negro and the stories of what happened to coloured men taken prisoner of war were very grim and of course believed by all of us implicitly.'

At the end of the war, Manley was back in London and in Hyde Park on Armistice Day along with a crowd of a million people. He was one of 37 West Indian soldiers to be awarded the Military Medal for bravery in action. But under the strain of the war and the shock of his brother's death he had a nervous breakdown. He returned to Oxford, however, and in 1919 continued his legal studies in London, spending nearly three years using Gray's Inn and its common room: 'I never came to know a single white man there or to speak to

Lawyer Manley

any except to say "Good Morning" or "Good day". I felt race hostility or suspicion moving around in lodging houses or shops. I saw clearly what was happening.'

In 1921 Manley married his cousin Edna, whose father was an English pastor and her mother Jamaican. She later became the most famous sculptor in Jamaica with an international reputation. In 1922 they returned to Jamaica where Manley became the foremost lawyer in the country and in the West Indies. In the Second World War, their son Michael enlisted in the Royal Canadian Air force to train as a wireless operator and gunner. Norman Manley died in 1969, but in 1972 Michael became Prime Minister of Jamaica in a landslide victory.

Again in the Second World War Britain relied heavily on Commonwealth troops to fight against Germany. Around 6,000 non-white volunteers served in the Royal Air Force and around 500 of these were young men recruited from the Caribbean. One of the most famous was **Cy Grant**, who became a household name in the late 1950s when he appeared on the BBC's *Tonight* programme singing topical calypsos. He was the first black person to appear regularly on British television.

Cyril Ewart Lionel Grant was born in Guyana in 1919, the great-grandson of a slave. His father was a Moravian minister, originally from Barbados, and his mother, who came from Antigua, was a music teacher with Scottish and East Indian heritage. He describes his upbringing: 'I was brought up in a typically colonial way, singing *Rule Britannia* and learning about English history and geography, but not knowing anything about the country I was born in. I knew as a young person in

Cy Grant (1919-2010)

Guyana that something was wrong. I felt frustrated by the colonial way of life. I knew that the colony was too small to hold me.'

Grant's way out came in 1941 when he joined the RAF. He trained in England and in 1943 qualified as a navigator and was commissioned as an officer. He joined a crew flying Lancaster bombers over Germany during the Battle of the Ruhr, but on his third operation the plane was shot down over Holland. The crew bailed out and Grant landed safely, but was captured by the Germans. They imprisoned him in Stalag Luft III, made famous in the films *The Great Escape* and *The Wooden Horse*.

Cy Grant was later moved to a huge POW camp in Lukenwalde, 50km south of Berlin, and in a poem he describes the cold, bug-infested conditions:

there's an awful stench in this room.
On three-tiered bunks we lie
prisoners
staring with vacant eye.

Nearing the end of the war, the Germans moved the prisoners again and again to evade the advancing Allied armies. The temperature that winter was -25C, one of the coldest on record, and the prisoners were freezing, soaked, famished and exhausted. Grant recalls being transported in boxcars: 'We lay on our sides, jammed like sardines hard against one another in two rows, facing each other with feet interlocking. The atmosphere was stifling and it was impossible to sleep. This seemed a great hardship, until I recalled the purgatory endured by slaves, my forebears, of the

Middle Passage, a journey of some six thousand miles. What was one night cramped like sardines in a cold boxcar, compared to weeks drowning in despair, vomit and excreta in the holds of a slave ship?'

They were eventually liberated by Russian soldiers, but still had to go out and look for cows to get something to eat. Grant describes what he saw: 'There were bodies of dead soldiers, mostly German, lying all around. In the gathering dusk, it was a grim sight; the brutal, futile, staring face of war. Unbelievably, this was the very first time I had come face to face with the stark horror of war – dead bodies, staring eyes, blood and mud and broken limbs and lives. We, the eagles, had dropped bombs from above, devastated towns and factories, killed, crippled and maimed thousands of men, women and children, but never witnessed the horrors of our own actions. We scurried over the bodies, lying there in the mud, eyes averted.'

After the war Cy Grant qualified as a barrister in 1950 but was unable to find work at the Bar, so was 'forced to find employment in show business'. In 1965 he acted as Othello at the Phoenix Theatre in Leicester, the first black person to play the part since Paul Robeson. In 1974 Grant founded the Drum Arts Centre as a showcase for black acting talent and in 2006 launched the Caribbean Aircrew Archive as a permanent record of West Indian volunteers who served in the RAF. He died in 2010, aged 90.

One of Cy Grant's fellow airmen was **Arthur Wint** from Jamaica, who in 1942, at the age of 22, joined the British Commonwealth Air Training Plan in Canada and was then sent to Britain in the summer of 1944 as a Flying Officer. In March 1945 he began piloting

Arthur Wint (1920-1992) in his RAF uniform

Spitfires and an accident in north Wales led to the rumour that he had been killed. The incident is described in the book *The Longer Run*, written by his daughter Valerie: 'He had been flying a Spitfire and had landed in the slipstream of a Lancaster Bomber. The air sucking behind the big plane tipped him up so that he landed nose-down, damaging the nose and wing tip. However, in order to get over the shock of that crash and to ensure he did not lose his nerve, the ground crew pulled him out of the plane, put him in another one and sent him right back up.' Wint's wife also came to England in 1943, where she joined the ATS and worked in a munitions plant and depot preparing for motor transport and parts to be used on D-Day in June 1944.

The iconic photograph of Arthur Wint, on which the statue at the National Stadium is based

Arthur Wint, at over 6' 5", was also an amazing athlete and became Jamaica's first Olympic gold medalist, winning the 400 metres at the 1948 Games, which took place in London only a few weeks after the *Windrush* arrived. The band of the RAF played the national anthem as the gold medal was hung around his neck.

In 1947 Wint left the RAF to attend St Bartholomew's Hospital as a medical student. In 1953 he graduated as a doctor and in 1955 returned to work in Jamaica. He settled in Hanover where he was the only resident doctor and treated the poor for free. He also served as Jamaica's High Commissioner in the UK from 1974-78.

Another comrade-in-arms was **Billy Strachan**, a Jamaican descended from a family of slaves, who was born in 1921. At the age of 18, only three months after leaving school, he decided to join the RAF and describes how he managed to sail to England: 'I was asked to pay a reduced fare, from £45 to £15. I didn't even have £15. So I sold my bicycle and my saxophone and with the proceeds I had about £17, paid my £15, and got a ship, and left Jamaica with about £2.10s. a small case with one change of clothes. That's how I came to England.'

After 12 weeks training as a wireless operator and air gunner, he was made a sergeant and joined a squadron of bombers making nightly raids over Germany. After 30 tours he was entitled to a job on the ground, but instead he applied for pilot training and after only seven hours' training was allowed to fly solo.

Strachan was promoted to first flying officer and then to flight lieutenant, when he was assigned his own batman, as he recalls: 'The batman was a very smooth Jeeves type and exactly the kind of character I had been led to expect. Meanwhile, I was just a little coloured boy from the Caribbean and I instinctively called him Sir. "No, Sir" the batman hastily corrected, "It is I who call you Sir".'

Billy Strachan was a daredevil pilot and was famous for his hair-raising but clever way of escaping German fighters: 'The trick was to wait until the enemy was right on your tail and, at the last minute, cut the engine, sending your lumbering Lancaster into a plunging dive, letting the fighter overshoot harmlessly above.'

On his fifteenth trip, however, his nerve finally snapped before he had even left Lincolnshire: 'I remember so clearly. I was carrying a huge bomb destined for German shipping. Our flight path was directly over Lincoln city and its magnificent cathedral perched high on a hill. It was a foggy night, with visibility down to 100 yards. The climb to clear the cathedral spire was always difficult, particularly with a heavy bomb load. I asked my engineer to make sure we were on course to clear the spire on top of the cathedral tower. He replied: "We are just passing it." I looked out, shocked that the spire was not where I expected, below us, but just a very few feet beyond our wingtip. I hadn't seen the spire at all – and I was the pilot! There and then my nerve went. I knew I couldn't go on – this was the end of me as a pilot! I flew out to sea, dropped my bomb load and flew back to the airfield.'

After the war Strachan trained as a lawyer and built a powerful reputation, becoming senior clerk to the

Billy Strachan (1921-1998) in his RAF uniform

magistrates in courts all over London. He wrote several important legal guides on subjects such as drink-driving and adoption. He also joined the Communist Party and became a leading figure in the anti-colonial struggle.

In 1948 Strachan was elected secretary of the London branch of the Caribbean Labour Congress which set up a committee to help the West Indians who had arrived on the *Windrush*, one of whom, C, G. Hemmings, wrote to Strachan: 'As one of the Jamaicans who came up on the *Windrush* I am in bad luck. Can't get a room to live all I try. Could you find me one. I would love a room with just a chair and a bed. See if you can help one that truly needs help.' Another, Kenneth Levy, wrote: 'A *Windrush* arrivee asking CLC for help, 27 years old with 4 years' service in the RAF in the UK with air traffic control.' In 1952 Strachan launched *Caribbean News*, one of the first left-wing newspapers for Caribbean people living in Britain, which was carried forward by Claudia Jones in 1958 with the *West Indian Gazette*.

Billy Strachan died in 1998, having been diagnosed with motor neurone disease. At his funeral a personal message from Janet Jagan was read out: 'Billy was my friend, my comrade, my mentor for most of my adult life. He gave himself fully to our struggles. He was a genuine Caribbean man always in the forefront of labour and political challenges of our region. I will miss him very much. Life without Billy is not the same.'

Don't Attack Iraq
Asher

Dem mek dem pack
To attack Iraq
But we counteract
Ca we nah go tek dat

Bush and Blair behaving
Like gutter rats
So now we have de gutter rats
We ha fe set a trap

Buss dem in dem head
Like David wid a sling shot
Buss dem in dem head
But Lord…
Buss dem wid de facts
For to tek youth life
Man a wickedness dat
Who is responsible fe dat?

Who will tek de blame
Who will tek de shame
You can't take another man's life
And do it in my name

So that is why we a complain
We nah sit pan we arse
An a drink champagne
We a write we letters
We a write dem wid complaints
We a post dem to de House of Parliament
Right away
Ca we want a serious word wid Mr Blair
We want to know
Why he can't feel despair

Now dem mek dem pack to attack Iraq
Like we no know wha dem a do behind we back
Selling arms to Iraq
Kick back an relax
A wha you call dat?
A hypocrite dat
But we done see through dat
Hear de gun dem a pop
An while you sleep in a you bed
Other lives in dread
An while you sleep in a you bed
Others live in dread

Your conscience dat must be dead
The life that living well that is ill-spent
You hide behind a regime
But the oil is your intent
That's what makes you content
Makes you just like Saddam himself

Now you mek you pack
To attack Iraq

But we a counteract
Ca we nah go tek that
Bush and Blair behaving
Like gutter rats
So now we have de gutter rats
We ha fe set a trap

Buss dem in dem head
Like David wid a sling shot
Buss dem in dem head
But Lord…
Buss dem wid de facts
For to tek youth life
Man a wickedness dat
Who is responsible fe dat?

Who will tek de blame
Who will tek de shame
You can't take another man's life
And do it in my name

SPORTSMEN

'For a black footballer originally from Guyana to have played in the very top teams in the world and be part of the Scottish influence which changed the nature of football in England and ultimately the rest of the world is truly remarkable.'

Tony Talburt *Andrew Watson: The World's First Black Football Superstar* 2017

Sir Learie Constantine, Knight Batchelor
Black Prince from the British Empire
Cricket was his life and through the game
The grandson of a slave came to fame
Born in Trinidad in all humility
He rose to the ranks of High Degree.

Cy Grant *Constantine Calypso* 1966

'Constantine's originality is a vital and full expression of the West Indian temperament. Constantine is cricket, West Indian cricket, just as Grace is English cricket.'

Neville Cardus *Good Days: A Book of Cricket* 1934

A West Indian immigrant who had an outstanding influence on British sport was the footballer **Andrew Watson**. In his biography Tony Talbut compares him to Lionel Messi and Cristiano Ronaldo, though he was a defender rather than a striker.

Watson was born in Georgetown, Guyana, in 1856, to a Scottish plantation owner named Peter Miller Watson and a local black woman named Hannah Rose. When slavery was abolished, Andrew's father received £800 in compensation for his 16 slaves. He sent his son to England for his education and Andrew then went on to Glasgow University, eventually becoming a qualified engineer. When his father died he left Andrew £35,000 in his will, the equivalent now of over £3m.

Andrew Watson played football for Queen's Park Football Club, the most dominant team in Scotland at the time, and later for the Corinthians, the top English club. He was the first black football administrator, as well as the first black player to win three national cup winners' trophies. In 1881 he captained Scotland in the team which beat England 6-1 at the Kennington Oval in London, in front of 8,600 spectators. This still remains England's heaviest defeat on home soil.

This was an era when football was still an amateur game and the rules and style of play were still developing. The English game was based on individual skills and the strength of the forwards. The

Andrew Watson (1856-1921) from Tony Talburt's book published in 2017

usual formation was 8 forwards and 2 defenders and the forwards would dribble en masse towards the opposition goal. In Scotland Watson and his teammates developed a team approach based on passing the ball, as opposed to just dribbling. Instead of 1-1-8, they adopted the 2-3-5 formation which lasted for nearly 100 years – two full-backs, three half-backs and five forwards. This was one of the reasons why, out of the first 15 internationals between England and Scotland, England won only one. These Scottish players had a great influence on the English game, as many of them moved south to play for teams in the north of England.

As Tony Talbut concludes: 'Even though he played as an amateur, Watson's achievements as a footballer could certainly rival, if not surpass, those of Arthur Wharton and Walter Tull. He played for the best national team at the time and also played for the two best amateur clubs in Britain.'

In July 2020 Malik Al Nasir (formerly Mark Watson) revealed that he had discovered he was related to Andrew Watson and had researched the family connections in Guyana. Malik grew up in care in Liverpool and also spent some time in an approved school in Manchester. He is now studying for a Ph.D. at Cambridge University researching the family history and writes: 'Andrew Watson was the first historical black role model I could be proud of. I wanted to know about his life.'

Just as Andrew Watson was instrumental in revolutionising the style of British football, so another Caribbean immigrant revolutionised the style of cricket. This was **Learie Constantine** from Trinidad. In his biography of Constantine, Peter Mason writes: 'His innings were dramatic and exhilarating, his bowling hostile and combative and his fielding quite simply the best there has ever been. He also laid a foundation stone for the greatness of West Indies cricketers to follow, from Sobers to Richards to Lara.'

Learie Constantine was born in Trinidad in 1901 and, although he left school at the age of 15, he had already been the school's cricket captain. His father was also a good cricketer and had toured England with the West Indies cricket team. Their ancestors were slaves, as Constantine writes in his book *Colour Bar*: 'I am black. My grandfather and grandmother were the children of slaves born into slavery.'

While touring England with the West Indies team in 1928, Constantine signed up for the Lancashire League, an amateur league, though each team was allowed one professional. He played for Nelson, a small textile weaving town of 40,000 people, 25 miles north of Manchester, which was called 'Little Moscow' because of its left-wing reputation. Constantine made Nelson the richest club in the league and was probably the best paid professional sportsman in 1930s Britain. In 1934 another club offered him a much higher fee than had been offered to Bradman, who was then at the height of his career.

The racism which Constantine initially experienced led him to consider leaving after his first year, but his wife Norma told him that they had made their decision and they were going to stick it out. In his book *Cricket Crackers* Constantine wrote: 'League crowds are largely composed of miners, mechanics, millworkers.' He concluded: 'If I have given some pleasure to

Learie Constantine (1901-1971)

Northern crowds, they have given me back ten times as much, by reassuring me over and over again that men are equal and King Cricket is master of us all.' C. L. R. James commented, 'League cricket today is what he made it.'

Constantine played for Nelson for nine seasons, in which they won the Championship seven times and were runners-up twice. In 1933 against Accrington he took all ten wickets for 10 runs in thirty-seven balls and in 1937 scored 192 not out against East Lancashire. Not only was he a brilliant batsman and bowler, but he was the consummate all-rounder. Bradman called him 'without hesitation' the greatest fielder he had ever seen. According to C. L. R. James he was 'probably the only all-rounder in cricket who could win his place in a Test side by fielding alone'. He had an encyclopedic knowledge of cricketers and cricket matches and wrote several books on the subject. After the Second World War he wrote that in 'modern Big Cricket' there is 'not enough red blood, swift fielding, hard hitting, hostile bowling and vigorous captaincy'. In *Cricket in the Sun* he predicted 'an increase in women's cricket' and foresaw the one-day game.

During the war he was employed by the Ministry of Labour as a Local Welfare Officer, responsible for the welfare of West Indians arriving to work in munitions factories in Liverpool. In 1944 he was involved in a famous incident when he was refused entry to a London hotel because he was black. He took the case to court and won damages. After the war, in 1954, Constantine finally qualified as a barrister, after eight years study.

Learie Constantine with Una Marson, broadcasting in 1942

He returned to Trinidad and from 1961 to 1964 served as high commissioner for Trinidad and Tobago. He was knighted in 1962 and became the first black peer in 1969. In his book *Colour Bar* (1954) he summed up his experience of Britain: 'Almost the entire population of Britain really expect the coloured man to live in an inferior area. Most British people would be quite unwilling for a black man to enter their homes, nor would they wish to work with one as a colleague, nor to stand shoulder to shoulder with one at a factory bench.'

His legacy is his contribution to West Indian cricket – what C. L. R. James called its 'newness', its 'independent style', which was largely due to 'the glamorous spontaneity of Constantine's cricket'. He adds, 'It was in the 1939 Test that Constantine played carefree, impudent cricket.' In 1940 *Wisden*, the cricketing bible, wrote, 'He revolutionised all the recognised features of cricket and surpassing Bradman in his amazing stroke play, he was absolutely impudent in his aggressive treatment of the bowling.' Constantine himself believed that the West Indies would 'preserve that naturalness and ease which distinguish our game'.

Jack London was born in Guyana in 1905, with a Scottish mother and Guyanese father. He was brought to England as a baby when his father, a teacher and church minister, came to London to train as a doctor. He later returned to Guyana, where he studied at the prestigious Queen's College, but came back to the UK as a teenager in 1920. He studied at the Regent Street Polytechnic where he joined the Polytechnic Harriers, one of the best athletics clubs, where Harry Edward also trained. Edward, whose mother was German and father Guyanese, became the only man to win the 100m, 220m and 440m in the AAA championship in 1922. (Later McDonald Bailey and Arthur Wint would also train with the Polytechnic Harriers.)

Jack London started competitive racing in 1924 and, at 6 feet 2 inches, he was also a great high jumper. In the 1928 Amsterdam Games he was the first black man to win an Olympic medal for Britain – the silver in the 100 metres. In the semi-final he equalled the Olympic record of 10.6 seconds. He also won a bronze medal in the 4 x 100m relay and was the first Olympic athlete to use starting blocks.

Jack London (1905-1966) equalling the Olympic 100m record in Amsterdam, 1928

In 1930 Jack London retired from the track with a leg injury and in the same year married Joyce Bonita at Marylebone register office. He later divorced and remarried Agnes Down, a dancer, in 1938. By this time he was working as a pianist and was an original member of the cast of Noel Coward's musical *Cavalcade* at the Theatre Royal in Drury Lane in 1931. He also appeared alongside the comedian Will Hay in the film *Old Bones of the River* in 1938.

After serving in the Army during the Second World War, Jack London wrote a coaching manual, entitled *The Way to Win on Track and Field*, in which he writes: 'I personally deplore the intrusion of the ultra-nationalistic element – with all its bickering and squabbles – and I think you will agree that in our sporting quests we British have the temperament to revel equally in our heritage, our team-work and our personal satisfaction at achievement.'

He also implores young athletes to look after their teeth: 'It does not take a doctor's knowledge to make any normally intelligent person realise that every decayed tooth is a miniature cesspool, adding its quota of slow poison to the system with every swallow, meal and drink that the owner takes. Today there is no excuse for not having your teeth properly attended to: the question of expense and clinical facilities are easily overcome. Do please realise that the initial discomfort in the dentist's chair is the alternative to the probability of lingering illness to come – and the inevitable reduction in your physical capacity.'

Jack London ended his days living in Marylebone Street and working as a porter in St Pancras Hospital. In 1966 he died of a stroke (subarachnoid haemorrhage). The secretary of the Polytechinc Harriers said of him: 'A man of great charm, shy and diffident, he would have been welcome at all times amongst us.'

The Talking Book
Asher

Reading a book is a political act
I wish someone had've told me that
I wish I had've known of the sacrifices made
So that I could simply sit, turn the page

It's only now that I am mature in age
Looking back at those mundane days
Sitting in classrooms bored out of my brains
Listening to teachers express in such an unexpressive way
The tiny words written on the academic page
That if understood would get me a job some day

Some day I won't need this place
Reading will take second place
I don't need words to conquer me
I will learn all I need from the streets
Till the streets taught me
That nothing in life is free
That every freedom that I have
Was earnt politically

Even the freedom of being able to read
Someone fought for that for me
So let us come together

Let us check out history
For the reality me a deal with
Is slavery

Now William Wells Brown
He knows what I mean
He wanted to read so bad
He couldn't even sleep
He used to bribe the white street children
With a lick of his sweet
Coz he knew being able to read
Would mean power, you see

See-saw, Marjorie Daw
Check out the man
Dem call him Gronniosaw

Now he, my friends
Was an African prince
Captured as a slave
Sailed on the slave ship
Observed his master reading to his crew
Decided he would like to do that too
But when he raised the book up to his ear
It never made a sound
So he went in search to find out
Where the secret could be found

What was the difference
Between the master and he
Why did not words jump out and speak
Maybe those words
Maybe they despise me

Can't you see how that's important
Can't you see how that is deep
I don't need no more than that
To try and convince me

That reading a book is a political act
I wish someone had've told me that
I wish I had've known of the sacrifices made
So that I could simply sit, turn the page.

WRITERS

Little comrade, never min'
Though a brother is unkin';
Treat him kindest as you can,
Show yourself the better man.

    Claude McKay *To a Comrade* 1912

'On coming to England the first impression the black man gets is that of utter loneliness.'

    Eric Walrond *The Negro in London* Black Man 1936

'I often wonder who I am and where is my country and where do I belong and why was I ever born at all.'

    Jean Rhys *Wide Sargasso Sea* 1966

And the sigh of that child
Is white as an orchid
On a crusted log
In the bush of Dominica

    Derek Walcott *Jean Rhys* 1980

Soon after the Second World War a number of West Indians came to Britain and became famous writers, for example the novelists Sam Selvon (Trinidad), and George Lamming (Barbados), poets like James Berry (Jamaica) and journalists such as Claudia Jones (Trinidad) and Donald Hinds (Jamaica). But there were also notable immigrant writers in the first half of the twentieth century.

One of the most famous was **Jean Rhys** who shot to fame in 1966 with the publication of *Wide Sargasso Sea*, which won the W. H. Smith Literary Award and also an award from the Royal Society of Literature. However, she had begun writing the novel 30 years earlier, after a visit to Dominica, and re-wrote it three times. The story derives from Charlotte Brontë's *Jane Eyre* and is an alternative account of Mr Rochester's mad wife Bertha Mason, now called Antoinette Cosway. As Rhys explains: 'Of course Charlotte Brontë makes her own world, of course she convinces you, and that makes the poor Creole lunatic all the more dreadful. I remember being quite shocked, and when I re-read it rather annoyed. "That's only one side – the English side" sort of thing. That unfortunate death of a Creole! I'm fighting mad to write *her* story.'

Jean Rhys actually came to England from Dominica as early as 1907, at the age of 16. Her father was a Welsh doctor and her mother a white Dominican of Scottish ancestry. She attended a Convent School run

Jean Rhys (1890-1979)

by Catholic nuns in which 'white girls were very much in the minority'. She describes her mother while also revealing her own concerns about her identity: 'She loved babies, any babies. Once I heard her say that black babies were prettier than white ones. Was this the reason why I prayed so ardently to be black, and would run to the looking-glass to see if the miracle had happened? And though it never had, I tried again. Dear God, let me be black.'

On her arrival in England Rhys spent a term at the Perse School in Cambridge where 'the bedrooms were unheated and I had already begun to shiver and shake'. She was asked about the West Indies, 'How do you get about then, if there are no trains, buses, cars or bicycles?' She replied, 'Horses, mules, carriages, buggies, traps.'

Rhys then enrolled in the Academy of Dramatic Art, later to become RADA, which was when she first read *Jane Eyre*. She describes her response to the tourist sites: 'I found St. Paul's bare and dull and Protestant, Westminster Abbey too crowded.' She 'simply hated' the Zoo, but was impressed with Ely Cathedral, 'I was so excited and moved that I began to tremble.' She sums up her feeling of isolation: 'I would never be part of anything. I would never really belong anywhere, and I knew it, and all my life would be the same, trying to belong, and failing. Always something would go wrong. I am a stranger and I always will be, and after all I didn't really care.'

Her abiding impression of the country was the cold: 'The cold the cold the cold. But I am not conquered yet. I do not cry myself to sleep yet.' In the index to her published letters (1931-1966) under 'weather, cold, rain, darkness, wind' there are 56 references! When discussing Rochester's mad wife, Rhys attempts to find out the 'reason why she tries to set fire to everything, and eventually succeeds', adding, 'Personally, I think *that* one is simple. She is cold – and fire is the only warmth she knows in England.'

While at the Academy, her father died and her mother could not afford to keep her there, so Rhys got a job in the chorus of a musical comedy and toured the country. Her experiences formed the basis of her novel *Voyage in the Dark*, published in 1934, though she had already written a book of short stories entitled *The Left Bank*, based on her time in Paris, which was published in 1927. During the First World War she worked in a railway canteen in London

After the publication of her novel *Good Morning Midnight* in 1939 Jean Rhys disappeared from the literary scene and her books went out of print. During the war she lived in rooms above a pub in Maidstone and wrote a diary in which she reminisces about her early days in England: 'I grew to hate London, to hate England. No one was ever kind to me.' She adds, 'Later on I learned to know that most English people kept knives under their tongues to stab me. No one told me, No one told me.'

In 1958, however, her latest novel was dramatised on the radio and she was traced to Cornwall. She began writing short stories again, which were published in various journals, and in 1966 *Wide Sargasso Sea* came out to wide acclaim. She was now living in Cheriton Fitzpaine in Devon and in a short story, published in 1976, she describes a cottage in Devon 'so meanly built, for poor people. Just four small rooms, and an attic. Like my life'. She bemoans 'the eternal drizzle' and the 'bullying treacherous wind'. Jean Rhys died, after a fall, in 1979 at the age of 88, while she was writing the beginning of an autobiography, which was published as *Smile Please*.

Unlike Jean Rhys, **Eric Walrond** was already a celebrated writer before he came to England. He was one of the stars in the Harlem Renaissance galaxy, which included his friends Langston Hughes, Zora

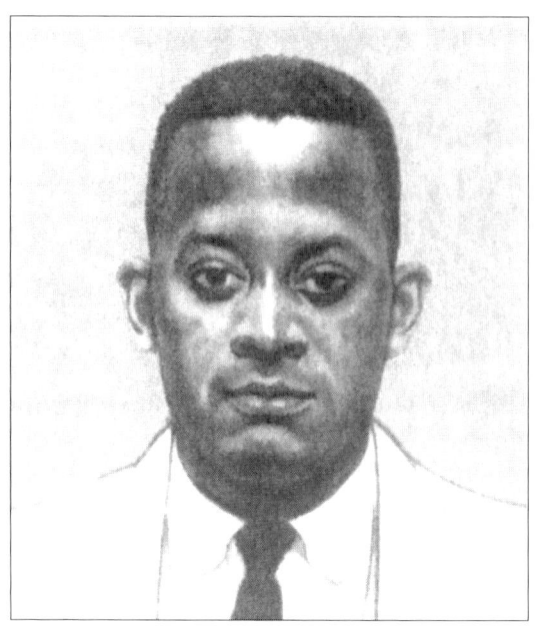

Eric Walrond (1898-1966)

Neal Hurston, and Claude McKay who also came from the Caribbean and visited England for a couple of years just after the First World War. Walrond's book of short stories *Tropic Death*, published in 1926, was reviewed by W. E. B. du Bois who called it a 'distinct contribution to Negro American literature' which shows 'with singular vividness the life of black laborers of the West Indies'. It was 'a human document of deep significance and great promise' showing 'truth and human sympathy'. The Jamaican historian Robert A. Hill wrote that it was 'probably the greatest short story work in the entire body of West Indian literature' and Langston Hughes said 'the throbbing life and sun-bright hardness of these pages fascinate me'. The book won Walrond three major awards, including the prestigious Guggenheim Foundation Fellowship in

1928, which funded him to 'travel and study in the West Indies' to prepare for a 'series of novels and short stories'. He was one of only three black writers among the 75 fellowship recipients.

Eric Walrond was born in Guyana in 1898 to immigrant parents from Barbados. After his father left the family in 1906, his mother took him to Barbados where they lived for five years before they went to Panama to try and join his father. Walrond was employed as a journalist on the *Panama Star and Herald* and learnt to speak Spanish fluently. In 1918 he left for New York where he became associate editor of Marcus Garvey's *Negro World*. He wrote numerous essays, reviews and short stories, which helped considerably in spreading the seeds of the Harlem Renaissance. He later commented on how West Indians were seen by African Americans in Harlem: 'The West Indian with his Scottish, Irish or Devonshire accent, was to the native Black who has still retained a measure of his African folk-culture, uproariously funny. He was joked at on street corners, burlesqued on the stage and discriminated against in business and social life.'

In 1933, after spending three years in Paris, Walrond travelled to London and in 1936 began to work for Marcus Garvey's *Black Man*, though he disagreed with much of Garvey's philosophy. He made contact with Harold Moody and Una Marson who invited him to write book reviews for *The Keys*. During this time Walrond had over 100 articles and reviews published, as well as numerous short stories and sketches. Then in 1939 at the outbreak of war he was one of the 1.5 million people evacuated from London in the first four days of September. He went to live in Bradford-on-Avon, a small town of 4,000 inhabitants, eight miles west of London, in Wiltshire.

During the war years he worked as a labourer for the Avon Rubber Company. In an article for the New York *Amsterdam News* (30 March 1940) he commented on the war which was meant to 'end the recurrent fear of Nazi aggression', but added 'such nobility of sentiment was also a feature of Britain's war aims in 1914-1918' when Britain happened to 'emerge with 1,415,929 square miles of new territory in Africa, Egypt, Cyprus, Palestine, Mesopotamia, New Guinea and Samoa, directly or indirectly under her control'.

After the war Walrond suffered from depression and in 1952 became a voluntary patient at Roundway Hospital in Devizes where he was instrumental in producing *The Roundway Review* 'to encourage free expression of ideas'. He was associate editor and a regular contributor. In *From British Guiana to Roundway*, for example, he praises the new National Health Service: 'Here at Roundway I've seen a hospital functioning not on voluntary contributions but under a N.H.S. – something I'd never seen before or ever dreamt of. Among my fellow patients I've seen some astonishing examples of brotherliness and self-sacrifice.' A short story, entitled *Strange Incident*, published in 1956 and set in Wiltshire, is seemingly autobiographical. He is accused by the U.S. military police of wearing U.S. army shoes. A constable asks him to remove one of his shoes to prove it's not stolen!

In 1957 Walrond discharged himself from hospital and moved back to London to research 'Negro poetry' at the British Museum, with the aim of putting on a performance by black actors, as he wrote, 'The programme should be up to date and none of the significant new voices should be overlooked.' On 5 October, 1958, only months after the Notting Hill race riots had taken place, *Black Unknown Bards* was performed at the Royal Court Theatre, but unfortunately, despite all Walrond's research, only African American poets were included.

Walrond spent the last years of his life working for an import-export firm near St Paul's Cathedral. George Lamming met him at the bar of a Jamaican night club, where he was a regular, and said, 'He was a very strong writer. It's a pity that something happened.' In 1966, just as he was negotiating the reissue of *Tropic*

Grave of Eric Walrond in Abney Park Cemetery, London

Death he had a heart attack and was buried without ceremony in Abney Park Cemetery in Stoke Newington, where his white gravestone has now turned green.

Before he died Walrond asked for the dedication in the reprint of his book to be changed to his three daughters, one of whom, Lucille, had become a teacher at the University of the West Indies and was a pioneer in the field of women's studies in the Caribbean. In 1969 another daughter, Jean, deposited a cheque for $850 at Barclay's Bank in Kingston, Jamaica. In his comprehensive study of Eric Walrond, published in 2015, James Davis writes that this was 'the first tangible benefit she and her sisters received from their father's writing. Finally, the literary labour he performed as a young man was profitable as he was headed for his grave; finally, he was providing for his daughters, from whom he had been estranged for forty years; finally, a West Indian family received royalties for a book by a West Indian about West Indians. Composed in Harlem, set in the Caribbean, and now profitable in London and Kingston, *Tropic Death* had traced a path across generations through the diaspora.'

A few months before his death Langston Hughes sent Walrond a Christmas card and one of his recent books, reminding him of their first meeting nearly half a century earlier. James Davis emphasizes his significance for post-war Caribbean literature: 'Walrond shared common experiences with other pre-*Windrush* intellectuals, such as C. L. R. James, George Padmore and Una Marson, forerunners to the West Indian writers who established a full-fledge literary movement after World War II.'

The most famous West Indian immigrant writer was **C. L. R. James** (who could also have been included amongst the political activists) and he was also the most versatile. In *Intellectuals in the Twentieth-century Caribbean*, Alistair Hennessy describes him as 'historian, novelist, literary critic, philosopher, journalist, raconteur, Pan-African and revolutionary socialist'. He could also have added dramatist, for in 1936 James's play about Toussaint L'Ouverture was performed at the Westminster Theatre in London, with Paul Robeson, whom James called 'the most remarkable human being I have ever met', in the leading role. In his collection of James's writings, *You Don't Play with the Revolution*, David Austin also notes the scope of his achievements: 'James made unique contributions to the study of a range of fields: history, political theory, literary criticism, drama, philosophy and sport.'

C. L. R. James was born to middle-class parents in Trinidad in 1901. Before coming to England he was a teacher at Queen's Royal College and had already showed promise as a writer, publishing five short stories and writing several articles on sport, as well as being involved in amateur dramatics, producing a number of plays such as *The Merchant of Venice* and *Othello*. He had also completed the novel *Minty Alley* which was eventually published in England in 1936.

James claimed that 'the first step to freedom was to go abroad' and on arrival in London in 1932 he spent 10 weeks acclimatizing himself to the city and its inhabitants. This resulted in a series of letters from London which were published in the *Port of Spain Gazette*. Like Jean Rhys, he visited the tourist attractions and commented, 'St. Paul's is very lovely indeed, but nowadays it is dwarfed by the modern monstrosities which overwhelm it on every side.'

He then spent nearly a year staying with his friend Learie Constantine to help him with his autobiography. He felt more comfortable in Nelson: 'I could forgive England all the vulgarity and all the depressing disappointment of London for the magnificent spirit of these north country working people.' He became the cricket correspondent for the *Manchester Guardian* and got more involved in politics, as he said, 'Cricket had plunged me into politics long before I was aware of it.'

As a Trotskyist, involved in the Independent Labour Party, James was in demand as a political speaker and he also spent some time in Paris researching the slave rebellion in San Domingo. This resulted in his monumental, ground-breaking book *The Black Jacobins*, published in 1938. In a lecture in Montreal in 1966, entitled *The Making of the Caribbean Peoples*, he refers back to these historic events: 'Let us go on with these extraordinary people, these West Indians. They won their freedom in 1803. Up to 1791 they had been slaves. All this was done within 12 years. They defeated a Spanish Army of some 50,000 soldiers, a British Army of 60,000 soldiers, and another 60,000 French men sent by Bonaparte to re-establish slavery. They fought Bonaparte's great army and drove it off their land.'

In 1938 James was invited to the USA for a lecture tour and also to visit Trotsky in Mexico. He married his second wife Constance Webb who, in her memoir *Not without Love,* described their first encounter when

C. L. R. James in Trafalgar Square, giving a speech at a rally for Ethiopia

James was giving a talk entitled *The Negro Question* in a Los Angeles church: 'From the wings strode a six-foot-three-inch, brown-skinned handsome man. His back was ramrod straight, his neck rather long, and he held his head slightly back, with chin lifted. There was an elegance and grace in his stance, and he looked like a prince or king. He was carrying books and an untidy sheaf of papers that he placed on the podium and never looked at again.'

C. L. R. James (1901-1989)

In 1949 their son Nobbie was born and in the 1950s, at the height of the McCarthyite witch-hunt against people with left-wing views, James was threatened with deportation as an illegal immigrant, which would have meant that he would never be allowed to return, so he decided to leave of his own volition. He promised to write regularly to his four-year-old son, resulting in *The Nobbie Stories for Children and Adults*, another of James's literary achievements.

So in 1953 he returned to England and after much further travelling finally settled in London in 1981 where he lived in Brixton until his death in 1989.

In *Beyond a Boundary*, his classic cricket book published in 1963, James described himself as 'a British intellectual long before I was ten, already an alien in my own environment among my own people, even my own family' and he maintained that Caribbeans 'were and had always been Western-educated'. Nevertheless in *Minty Alley* he had written a novel which was the precursor of many Caribbean novels to come, as Eugenia Collier points out in *Fifty Caribbean Writers*: 'In turning attention inward to the indigenous folk rather than outward to imposed cultural concepts, James helped to lay the foundation for a literature based upon West Indian truths, a West Indian vision of the world. He initiated a change of direction for his own generation and broke new ground for writers yet to come.'

In *Culture and Imperialism* Edward Said sums up the significance of migration in C. L. R. James's writing: 'His basic metaphor is that of a voyage taken by ideas and people; those who were slaves and subservient classes could first become the immigrants and then the principal intellectuals of a diverse new society.'

SELECT BIBLIOGRAPHY

Agard, John (2009) *Alternative Anthem*, Northumberland: Bloodaxe Books

Austin, David (2009) *You Don't Play with the Revolution*, Edinburgh: AK Press

Baku, Shango (2008) *Beacons of Liberation*, London: Hansib

Boswell, James (1791) The *Life of Samuel Johnson*, London: Charles Dilly

Bressey, Caroline & Hakim Adi (eds.) (2011) *Belonging in Europe – The African Diaspora and Work*, Abingdon: Routledge

Brinkhurst-Cuff, Charlie (ed.) (2018) *Mother Country*, London: Headline

Bundock, Michael (2015) *The Fortunes of Francis Barber: The True Story of the Jamaican Slave Who Became Samuel Johnson's Heir*, New Haven: Yale University Press

Cardus, Neville (1934) *Good Days: A Book of Cricket*, London: Jonathan Cape

Constantine, Learie (c1950) *Cricket Crackers*, London: Stanley Paul

Dance, Daryl Camber (ed.) (1986) *Fifty Caribbean Writers*, New York: Greenwood Press

Darwin, Charles (1871) *Descent of Man*, London: John Murray

Davis, James (2015) *Eric Walrond: A Life in the Harlem Renaissance and the Transatlantic Caribbean*, New York: Columbia University Press

Derry, J. F. (2010) *Darwin in Scotland: Edinburgh, Evolution and Enlightenment*, Dunbeath: Whittles Publishing

Donnell, Alison (2003) 'Una Marson: feminism, anti-colonialism and a forgotten fight for freedom' in Bill Schwarz (ed.) *West Indian Intellectuals in Britain*, Manchester: Manchester University Press

Edwards, Paul & David Dabydeen (1991) *Black Writers in Britain, 1760-1890*, Edinburgh: Edinburgh University Press

Ewing, Adam (2014) *The Age of Garvey: How a Jamaican Activist Created a Mass Movement and Changed Global Black Politics*, Princeton: Princeton University Press

Ferrari, Roberto C. (2014) 'Fanny Eaton: The "Other" Pre-Raphaelite Model', *PRS Review*, Volume XXII, Number 2

Fryer, Peter (1984) *Staying Power: The History of Black People in Britain*, London: Pluto Press

Gentleman, Amelia (2019) *The Windrush Betrayal: Exposing the Hostile Environment*, London: Guardian Books

Goodfellow, Maya (2019) *Hostile Environment: How Immigrants Became Scapegoats*, London: Verso

Gopal, Priyamvada (2019) *Insurgent Empire: Anticolonial Resistance and British Dissent*, London: Verso

Grant, Colin (2019) *Homecoming*, London: Vintage

Grant Cy (2006) *A Member of the Royal Air Force 'Of Indeterminate Race'*, Bognor Regis: Woodfield Publishing

Grant, Cy (2008) *Rivers of Time*, London: Naked Light

Green, Jeffrey (1987) 'John Alcindor (1873-1924): A Migrant Biography', *Immigrants and Minorities*, Volume 6, Number 2

Grimshaw, Anna (1992) *The C. L. R. James Reader*, Oxford: Blackwell

Horsley, David (2019) *Billy Strachan*, London: Caribbean Labour Solidarity
Hoyles, Asher (2018) *Raise Up the Low, Bring Down the Mighty*, Hertford: Hansib
Hoyles, Asher & Martin (2011) *Caribbean Publishing in Britain: A Tribute to Arif Ali*, Hertford: Hansib
Hoyles, Martin (2004) *The Axe Laid to the Root: The Story of Robert Wedderburn*, London: Hansib
Innes, Lyn (2002) *A History of Black and Asian Writing in Britain*, Cambridge: Cambridge University Press
James, C. L. R. (1936) *Minty Alley*, London: Secker & Warburg
James, C. L. R. (1938) *The Black Jacobins*, London: Secker & Warburg
James, C. L. R. (1963) *Beyond a Boundary*, London: Hutchinson
James, C. L. R. (1984) *At the Rendezvous of Victory: Selected Writings*, London: Allison & Busby
James, C. L. R. (1986) *Cricket*, London: Allison & Busby
James, C. L. R. (2003) *Letters from London: Seven Essays by C. L. R. James*, Port of Spain, Trinidad & Tobago: Prospect Press
Jarrett-Macauley, Delia (1998) *The Life of Una Marson 1905-65*, Manchester: Manchester University Press
Makalani, Minkah (2011) *In the Cause of Freedom: Radical Black Internationalism from Harlem to London*, Chapel Hill: The University of South Carolina Press
Makonnen, Ras (1973) *Pan-Africanism from Within*, London: Oxford University Press
Marson, Una (1937) *The Moth and the Star*, Kingston, Jamaica: The Author
Marson, Una (2011) *Selected Poems*, Leeds: Peepal Tree Press
Martin, Tony (2007) *Amy Ashwood Garvey*, Dover: The Majority Press

McKay, Claude (1933) *Banana Bottom*, New York: Harper and Brothers

Moody, Harold A. (1944) *The Colour Bar*, London: Mildmay Centre

Noble, E. Martin (1984) *Jamaica Airman: A black airman in Britain 1943 and after*, London: New Beacon Books Ltd.

Padmore, George (1936) *How Britain Rules Africa*, London: Wishart Books

Padmore, George (1937) *African and World Peace*, London: Martin Secker & Warburg

Parascandola, Louis J. (ed.) (1998) *'Winds Can Wake up the Dead': An Eric Walrond Reader*, Detroit, Michigan: Wayne State University Press

Prince, Mary (1993) *The History of Mary Prince, a West Indian Slave, Related by Herself*, Ann Arbor: University of Michigan Press

Rastogi, Pallavi & Jocelyn Fenton Stitt (eds.) (2008) *Before Windrush: Recovering Asian and Black Literary Heritage within Britain*, Newcastle: Cambridge Scholars Publishing

Rhys, Jean (1927) *The Left Bank*, London: Jonathan Cape

Rhys, Jean (1934) *Voyage in the Dark*, London: Constable & Co.

Rhys, Jean (1939) *Good Morning Midnight*, London: Constable & Co.

Rhys, Jean (1984) *Letters 1931-66*, (edited by Francis Wyndham & Diana Melly) London: André Deutsch

Rhys, Jean (1990) *Smile Please: An Unfinished Autobiography*, London: Penguin

Said, Edward (1993) *Culture & Imperialism*, London: Chatto & Windus

Seacole, Mary (1984) *Wonderful Adventures of Mrs Seacole in Many Lands*, Bristol: Falling Wall Press

Sherlock, Philip (1980) *Norman Manley*, London: Macmillan

Smith, John Thomas (1883) *Mendicant Wanderers through the Streets of London*, Edinburgh: William P. Nimmo

Talburt, Tony (2017) *Andrew Watson: The World's First Black Football Superstar*, Hertford: Hansib

Teelucksingh, Jerome (2013) *Caribbean Liberators*, Palo Alto, C. A.: Academic Press

Walrond, Eric (1926) *Tropic Death*, New York: Boni & Liveright

Wint, Valerie (2012) *The Longer Run: A Daughter's Story of Arthur Wint*, Kingston: Ian Randle Publishers